AFFIRMATIVE

WHY YOU CAN SAY YES TO THE BIBLE AND YES TO PEOPLE WHO ARE LGBTQI+

JONATHAN TALLON

RICHARDSON JONES
—— PRESS ——

ISBN (paperback): 978-1-7392616-0-3

ISBN (ebook): 978-1-7392616-1-0

CONTENTS

1. Introduction   1
2. What does the Bible say about homosexuality?   9
3. How should we apply the Bible when our culture is different?   17
4. Adam and Steve (and Eve and Niamh)   23
5. Leviticus, commandments and a new commandment   29
6. The sin of Sodom   39
7. The silence of the gospels   43
8. Reading Romans the right way   53
9. The context of Corinth   71
10. Jude the obscure   79
11. What does the Bible say about transgender people?   83
12. An inclusive Bible   95
13. Learning from history   107
14. Conclusion   117
Postscript   123
Appendix   125

A note on language   153
Acknowledgments   157
Copyright - Scriptural passages   159

CHAPTER 1
INTRODUCTION

IF YOU ARE an evangelical Christian who is confused or conflicted by the debates over sexuality and gender, then this book is for you.

Let me sketch a situation, and see if it sounds familiar to you.

You are sitting in your church on a Sunday. You have brought along a non-Christian friend you got to know through sport. The worship band has finished playing, and the preacher gets up to start the sermon. They say that they are going to address the topic of same-sex marriage, and how sinful it is.

How do you feel?

Some of us may feel confident and relieved. At last, the preacher is meeting the world's agenda head on. The church is called to be countercultural. Your friend will realise that this church means business for God.

But not all of us will feel that way. Some of us may feel nervous. Questions may start running through our heads. What will the preacher say? Will my friend think that the church is bigoted, or prejudiced? Will they want to come back? What if my friend is gay?

Alongside that nervousness may be embarrassment. You

want your friend to experience a place that cares about love and justice, and fear that they will not see past the preacher's position on sexuality.

After the service, after your friend has returned to their home, perhaps you will also be feeling conflicted. You work in places where equality is seen as normal, where people can be openly gay and no one questions it. Maybe some of your colleagues are in marriages or long-term partnerships with the same sex. Or maybe a colleague or family member has transitioned from one gender to another.

And yet, all of this becomes problematic as soon as you enter the church doors. Some churches denounce your colleagues' relationships as symbols of all that is wrong with the world, while others maintain an embarrassed silence over the whole matter.

You find yourself conflicted.

And that conflict arises because you care deeply about two separate issues.

You know the importance of scripture; that it is God-breathed. You have been inspired, taught and challenged by God through the Bible throughout your Christian journey.

But you also care deeply for your friends, family, colleagues and others who are lesbian, or gay, or bisexual, or trans, or queer, or intersex, or otherwise identifying in a way that is not heterosexual or cisgender.

Additionally, you yourself may identify as one of these, and the conflict is internal to your very identity.

Some people express this feeling as being a conflict between your head and your heart. Your head says that the Bible condemns homosexuality, so it must be wrong, while your heart longs for good news for people who are LGBTQI+.

In reality, of course, both your love for scripture and your love for people who are LGBTQI+ involve both head and heart. The conflict is real at every level.

I would like to point out something positive here about that tension. That sense of conflict is healthy. It shows you care. If you did not, the tension would not arise. You want the church to be a beacon of light to a world in need, and you want to love, care for and respect those around you.

The conflict arises because many of us have been told that the Bible condemns homosexuality and transitioning or not conforming to gender norms. You seem to be left with only two stark choices: accept scripture, and condemn homosexuality and being transgender; or reject scripture and accept those that are homosexual and transgender.

But those are not the only two choices.

In this book, you will see how and why you can say 'yes': 'yes' to the Bible and 'yes' to affirming those who are gay, lesbian, bi or trans.

In many conversations, I have found a number of barriers that block being able to say that double 'yes'. For you, the main stumbling block may be certain verses in the Old and New Testaments that seem to condemn homosexuality. Even if you could be persuaded of a broad theme of acceptance in the Bible, these verses remain an issue.

These verses are sometimes known as the 'clobber' verses by those who are affirming. It is not too difficult to guess why they ended up with this nickname.

Sometimes, those on the affirming side will point out that these verses are only a handful out of over thirty thousand verses in the Bible. You can find plenty more verses about money and injustice.

That is true. Perhaps we need to recalibrate our priorities to match closer those of the Bible.

Even so, it is not enough simply to ignore these verses. They are part of scripture, and deserve serious treatment and attention.

In this book, therefore, you will find chapters on the following verses or passages:

- Genesis 1 and 2
- Genesis 19 (the story of Sodom and Gomorrah)
- Leviticus 18:22 and 20:13
- Matthew 19:4–6
- Romans 1:26–27
- 1 Corinthians 6:9 & 1 Timothy 1:10
- Jude 7

Before we examine these passages in detail, though, we first need background on some of the differences between the times and cultures in which the Biblical books were written, and the dominant approach that we have now in western culture. If we are unaware of these differences, it can mislead us as we seek to understand what the issues were.

We also need to consider how we interpret the Bible. Generally, it is perfectly fine to draw lessons from scripture for guidance for our own lives without considering too carefully how we are doing this. But when it comes to important, sensitive and potentially divisive issues like sexuality and gender, we need to be a little more self-aware. I have therefore included a chapter on how we apply the Bible.

The 'clobber' verses only cover the issue of sexuality. However, this book is also advocating for the affirmation of people who are transgender. So, you will find a chapter on the Bible and people who are transgender.

Often, at this point in my work, I am asked whether the Bible has anything positive to say, whether the Bible can affirm (rather than merely being silent). This can be another barrier for some people. I believe that the Bible has a strong message of inclusion, and I explain why in its own chapter.

We also need to be aware of our history. Whilst debates

around sexuality and gender may be new, the church has faced divisive issues many times over the last two thousand years. In the hope that we can learn from history, I consider one such issue—slavery—that the church has faced in the past, to see what lessons we might apply to today.

As you read through, you may notice that there are no footnotes or endnotes. I rarely quote directly from academic journals or books.

This is deliberate, to make the book accessible and easier to read. However, all the material is based on extensive academic scholarship. You can find a brief guide to some of the most relevant articles and books for each chapter in the appendix. I also cover one or two issues in greater depth there. For those who wish to follow up on the scholarship themselves, I also maintain an annotated bibliography at my website, which you can find at the link below:

www.bibleandhomosexuality.org/bibliography/

I do use one common abbreviation: LGBTQI+. This stands for lesbian, gay, bisexual, transgender, queer, or intersex, and the plus covers the various other sexualities and genders (for example, pansexual, asexual). While each group faces separate and distinct issues (and each group in turn is diverse), all face discrimination based on sexuality or gender.

You may also want to know something about me. Am I only writing this to justify my own identity? What qualifications do I have to say anything on the topic?

All of us come to this area with a background of experiences and life which has shaped us and which in turn affects how we shape what we say and think. So, to enable you to place this book in some type of context, here is a little about my background.

I made a commitment to Christ when I was fourteen, having had a background where my family went to church weekly. At university, I was an active member of the Christian

Union. Once I started work, I joined an inner-city evangelical church in Manchester, where I was involved with youth work. Feeling called by God to ministry in the Church of England, I studied at St. John's College in Nottingham, which was in the open evangelical tradition.

Once ordained, I was a curate in Bury before becoming a vicar in an urban parish to the west of Manchester.

For over a decade, I have been a biblical studies tutor at an ecumenical theological college in Manchester, where many of our mature students are training for ordained ministry in the non-conformist tradition. I have taught a range of modules at undergraduate and postgraduate level, and have also been the research programme leader.

I am married with three children. I currently attend a large evangelical church close to my home in Manchester.

Why did I write this book? I began teaching about the Bible and sexuality to people training for Baptist ministry in 2010. At the same time, I was teaching postgraduate modules on Paul's letter to the Romans. It became clear that there were few straightforward guides to help people consider whether you could be faithful to the Bible and affirm LGBTQI+ people. This was before Matthew Vines had published *God and the Gay Christian*, or Colby Martin *Unclobber* (both are good books, by the way).

There seemed to be two sides in the debate: Christians with a high regard for scripture who were non-affirming; and Christians with a lower regard for scripture who were affirming. But I was in a third place: taking scripture seriously and affirming.

My teaching material gave students and ministers in training a basis for how to hold scripture and affirmation together. In time, I began to be invited to churches and gatherings of ministers to help them consider the Bible and sexuality.

A sabbatical gave me the opportunity to create web-based resources: a website and YouTube channel. These have reached over a hundred thousand people, and some have been kind enough to tell me how helpful they have found the material.

This book is based loosely on that material developed and sharpened by interacting with many students and others over the years since I began teaching in this area. My hope is that more people may find this helpful in their journey with Christ.

As to my views on the subjects of sexuality and gender, I have held them for a long time. There has been no dramatic encounter, no damascene conversion. I have friends who are gay, and friends who have transitioned, and I am grateful for knowing part of their stories. Their experiences strengthen my conviction that affirming those who are LGBTQI+ is the right, just and loving approach, but those experiences were not the cause of that conviction.

Simply put, I am affirming because I believe it is right, and I offer here in this book some of the reasons why you can say yes to the Bible and yes to people who are LGBTQI+.

CHAPTER 2

WHAT DOES THE BIBLE SAY ABOUT HOMOSEXUALITY?

THE BIBLE SAYS nothing about homosexuality.

If that is true, you may be wondering what is in the rest of the book. Is it just going to be blank page after blank page?

Let me qualify that first statement: the Bible says nothing about homosexuality *directly*.

In this chapter, you are going to find out why I make this statement, why it is not obvious to us today, and what that means for us when we use the Bible to find guidance about the inclusion of people who are LGBTQI+.

Most of the time, my problem with the Bible is not trying to understand it but trying to follow it in my daily life. Thankfully, we only need to remember two commands: love God; and love our neighbours. They are simple and straightforward to understand. But following them—that is another story. I keep on trying to love God and neighbour, and (like all of us) keep on failing, and keep on having to throw myself on the mercy of God.

Here, *understanding* is the straightforward part; it is the *doing* that is hard. So much so, that we need God's grace.

And because much of the time our problem is in following through in our lives rather than understanding the Bible, the grand Protestant tradition developed which expected everyone, not just priests or academics, to read scripture, and rely on its plain meaning.

This is part of the inheritance of the Baptist tradition, where members meet together to discern together the mind of Christ.

It is the tradition of Wycliffe, who first translated the Bible into English, and Tyndale, who hoped that a boy ploughing the field would know scripture, and countless others since.

And, most of the time, expecting to be able simply to read the Bible and find the plain meaning of scripture is right.

Most of the time...

But not in the area of sexuality.

If we apply our modern, cultural understanding of sexuality when we read the Bible, it will mislead us.

Occasionally, we can get tripped up, and not even realise that what we think is the 'plain meaning' of a passage is poles apart from how people in the first century would have understood it.

In many areas, the past is like the present. Humans haven't changed much in the last two thousand years. We still get angry, fall in love, like to play, show off, gossip, tell jokes and do all the countless activities that humans have done for generations.

However, in some areas large shifts have occurred. The differences in cultural understandings of sexuality between ancient Romans and today's western cultures is immense.

Let me explain.

When we think about sexuality, we usually think about to whom you are attracted: someone of the opposite gender; or your own. We have a specific term for this: sexual orientation. We use *heterosexual* for those attracted to the opposite gender; *homosexual*, *gay* or *lesbian* for those attracted to the same gender; and *bisexual* or *pansexual* for those attracted to both or across the whole gender spectrum. And there are a range of terms beyond these.

So, if I said, 'Keith is homosexual', then you might expect him to be attracted to other men, and perhaps to be in a relationship with a man, or maybe married to a man.

And then you open up your Bible, and read 1 Corinthians 6:9, and see a reference to 'homosexual offenders' (NIV, 1978 ed.) or 'homosexual perverts' (GNB). Someone then suggests you read Romans 1:27, and when you find this passage you read about men committing indecent acts with other men.

The plain meaning of scripture seems to be staring you in the face.

Maybe you would like it to be otherwise. Perhaps you do not understand why the Bible seems to say it is wrong. But it is there. In black and white. The plain meaning of scripture.

The Bible appears to say, plainly, that being homosexual—gay or lesbian—is not OK.

But not all is as it seems.

The ancient Roman approach to understanding sexuality was completely different from ours—and those passages do not mean what you might assume.

This is how different the ancient Roman worldview is from our own.

Picture a typical, happily married Roman man—let us call him Fabius. Fabius is the master of his household. He has a loving wife, with whom he enjoys a full relationship, both emotionally and physically. They have three children, and Fabius is a respected member of society.

Fabius, besides intercourse with his wife, also regularly rapes his male and female slaves (of all ages), rapes boys if the opportunity presents itself, and frequently attends a local brothel where he has intercourse with prostitutes (some of whom are boys who are enslaved).

None of these actions affects his reputation (whether or not they are brought to light). His masculinity, his sexuality, and his honour remain untouched. As I said, he is a respected member of society.

In ancient Rome, sexuality was not defined by which gender you had sex with, or to which gender you were attracted, but whether or not you were the dominant, active, penetrating partner.

So long as a freeborn man like Fabius was the dominant partner, little else mattered, provided you did not sleep with someone else's wife or daughter. Enslaved people and prostitutes did not count.

It mattered little who you were with, but it mattered whether you were in charge.

To be the dominant, active, penetrating partner was to be virile and manly. To be the passive partner—to be penetrated—was to be weak and effeminate.

In particular, and most alien to our own Western culture, pederasty (intercourse with enslaved boys by men) was commonplace. It was not prohibited either legally or socially, but was simply, tragically, part of everyday life.

In fact, if Fabius wanted to prove his masculinity, he could do that through aggressive sex with an enslaved person—whether male or female. Boys, typically between the ages of ten to eighteen, were seen as equally as desirable as women. It wasn't until they started to grow a beard that they become off-limits.

As you can imagine, this means that same-sex activity by an adult male was practically always abusive. As an example, the Roman poet Martial uses the term 'cut to pieces' for the passive partner. They were seen as 'used, humiliated, and physically and morally damaged' (Ruden, 2010, 49). The active partner could carry on, using boys and then discarding them as they grew older. It is telling that there is no Roman word for 'homosexual', but there are two different terms (*deliciae* and *concu-*

binus) for the enslaved boy kept precisely for the purpose of being abused sexually by his master.

Let us be clear. If, in the ancient Roman empire, you talked about men having sex with males, everyone would have understood you to mean men raping and abusing boys, many of which were enslaved.

This may both surprise and shock you. Surely there were same-sex couples? Weren't there loving gay and lesbian couples? If human nature hasn't changed, it stands to reason that some people back then must have been gay or lesbian as we understand it today.

I am sure there were people 2,000 years ago who were gay or lesbian. And I am also sure that some formed adult, loving relationships.

But, with a few scattered exceptions, they mostly remained hidden from the rest of society. If the couple's secret became known, it would destroy the reputation and honour of at least one of the couple. Sexuality was understood hierarchically, so one of the partners would be seen as the passive partner and disgraced.

This is why most of the evidence we do have of ancient same-sex relationships come from private material: charms; spells; and graffiti. Sometimes it also comes from the insults of others.

But there simply was not the cultural space for an open, equal, committed relationship between adult males or females in ancient Rome in New Testament times.

In today's Western societies, pederasty is (rightly) condemned, and adult loving same-sex relationships are mainly accepted (at least legally). This is the opposite to Roman times, where pederasty was accepted, and a male having intercourse with an adult male was not.

You may find this hard to accept, so alien is this cultural

approach from ours. But it is an established finding of how the ancient Roman world worked.

This is why Jewish criticisms of male same-sex activity in Roman times assumed that one of the participants would be a boy; in other words, they condemned pederasty.

Here is an example from Philo of Alexandria, who lived about the same time as St. Paul, and who, like Paul, was Jewish.

> 'And let the man who is devoted to the love of boys submit to the same punishment, since he pursues that pleasure which is contrary to nature...'

> — PHILO, *SPECIAL LAWS* 3.39

It was not just the Jewish communities that attacked this practice. The earliest Christians also condemned pederasty as something routinely accepted by society but rejected by the Church. The earliest interpretation of Romans 1:26–7 that we have comes from Athenagorus, a second century Christian. He assumes that Paul is talking about pederasty:

> 'For those who have set up a market for fornication and established infamous resorts for the young for every kind of vile pleasure, who do not abstain even from males, males with males committing shocking abominations... ...These adulterers and pederasts defame the eunuchs and the once-married...'

> — ATHENAGORAS, *APOLOGY* 34

This assumption continues throughout the first centuries of the Church. Writer after writer, from Justin Martyr to Gregory of Nazianzus, condemns pederasty, calling it 'child corruption'.

This, therefore, is the background to the world of the New

Testament. It was a world where a freeborn man like Fabius was expected to display his masculinity and dominance through intercourse, not just with his wife, but also with those he enslaved and prostitutes, regardless of whether they were male or female.

This is why using the term 'homosexuality' is misleading when we apply it to the New Testament.

First, the ancient world was generally uninterested in questions of orientation—whether it was males or females to whom you were attracted—but much more concerned with what you did: action rather than orientation.

Secondly, there was no term in either Latin or Greek for 'homosexual person'. All the terms used defined people based on whether they were the active, dominant person or the passive, submissive person.

Thirdly, if anyone referred to an adult male having intercourse with males, everyone would assume that the males were boys, or enslaved. They would also assume that the relationship was one between power and lack of power, and that the boy would be humiliated.

But what would *not* be assumed is that the adult male only had intercourse with boys. Others would expect the man also to have intercourse with women (enslaved people and prostitutes) as well as being married or expecting to be married in the future.

How should this affect our reading of scripture? At the least, in this complex area, it might stop us from misleading appeals to the 'plain meaning of scripture'.

Whenever we look at Biblical passages about sex, the wider context was one where male same-sex activity was generally assumed to be pederasty—the abuse of boys. Once we recognise this as the background, it raises issues as to how we apply scriptures written in a sexual cultural content so vastly different from our own.

The next chapter explores in more detail how we handle situations where our context differs from that of biblical times. Sexuality is just one of a number of controversial areas with which, over the centuries, the Church has had to grapple. We take a look back at how the Church has handled these situations before.

Later chapters examine particular verses in much more depth, including 1 Cor. 6:9–10 and Romans 1:26–27. But as you read through them, bear in mind the point of this chapter. Whilst in our modern world, terms like 'homosexuality' might conjure up images of loving couples of the same gender in long term relationships, the ancient world was different. The world of the New Testament had no word for homosexuality, and precious little visibility of anything like same-sex couples today. In the ancient world, male-male sex meant pederasty. It meant abuse. It meant rape. Married men were the abusers; the abused were usually enslaved people or prostitutes.

The ancient world's culture was condemned for this in its time, first by Jewish people, and then by Christians. I would hope all Christians would still condemn it now.

So what does the Bible, written in this ancient world, have to say about homosexuality? As we understand homosexuality today, of loving, equal relationships, it says nothing directly at all.

CHAPTER 3

HOW SHOULD WE APPLY THE BIBLE WHEN OUR CULTURE IS DIFFERENT?

'THE BIBLE CONDEMNS HOMOSEXUALITY'. You will have heard this, and you will not be surprised to know that I disagree. As the previous chapter outlined, the same-sex activity that was publicly discussed in the ancient world mainly had pederasty in view. However, some will still argue that the Bible condemns all forms of same-sex activity, whether or not the particular focus was pederasty. And if the Bible condemns homosexuality, then we too should condemn it. That is how we are taught to apply the Bible. We must do it lovingly, but if we take the word of God seriously, we have no choice.

It is a compelling argument on the face of it. This is often how we use the Bible to make ethical decisions. For example:

- The Bible condemns murder.
- Therefore, we should condemn murder.

And who is going to disagree with that? However, let us try the same logic with a different topic.

Do you have a mortgage? Or perhaps a car-loan? Maybe you use a credit card, or are slowly paying back student loans.

All of these are forms of loans. Let us apply the Bible to these situations.

- The Bible condemns moneylending.
- Therefore, we should condemn mortgages, interest-paying savings accounts, car-loans, student loans and credit cards.

Yet, we do not. Have you ever heard a sermon railing against couples taking out mortgages to buy their first house? Have you read Christian books denouncing those who possess credit cards? You may have heard sermons about abusive moneylending, where loan sharks prey on vulnerable people, but not moneylending in general. You may have campaigned for or wanted student loan debt to be forgiven, but not on the principle that loans are, in themselves, wrong.

I have been going to church all my life, and I have never heard a sermon on any of these topics.

Why is that? The logic seems impeccable.

Some of you may be questioning the Bible's stance on moneylending. Does it really condemn it?

Before the reformation, about 500 years ago, the Church universally held that moneylending was wrong, and that this was a clear teaching of the Bible. The old term for moneylending is usury. The Church considered it a mortal sin (for those who are not used to sins being classified, this is the worst category).

How seriously did the Church take moneylending? If you lent money for profit, you could not get a Christian burial.

This approach continued into the reformation. For example, Martin Luther denounced lending money for profit, seeing it as wicked.

If, for 1500 years, the Church uniformly thought moneylending was unbiblical and immoral, how has Christian thought shifted so radically?

The reason, at least in part, is because of the thinking of the great protestant reformer, Calvin.

The time of the reformation was a time of change, and this included the economy. People began to question whether moneylending in all circumstances was always wrong. Claude de Sachin, a friend of Calvin's, asked him in 1545 for advice on whether lending money for interest could ever be considered not sinful, and received a carefully crafted reply.

Calvin proposed that, in certain circumstances, it might *not* be sinful to lend money. This was an incendiary idea, and the letter remained private until a decade after Calvin's death. But how did he reach his conclusion?

His answer covered a range of areas. Calvin considered the authority of the Bible compared with interpretations of the Bible. He emphasised the need to understand what the writings meant in their original context and to their original audience. He suggested that you need to look behind prohibitions in the Bible to see their purpose. Above all, the question of how this fitted in with justice and love needed to be addressed.

Calvin recognised that the Bible's context and his own context, in 16th century Geneva, were radically different from each other.

He argued that the Bible was addressing moneylending that was oppressive and harmful to the poor. This was potentially different from a business borrowing money to invest, where a loan could benefit both the lender and the borrower.

In other words, the Biblical prohibitions were addressing a situation different enough from that in Geneva, that in some circumstances it could be fine to lend money for profit.

The reasoning of Calvin (and others at the time) is why you, like me, have never sat through a sermon on the evils of having a mortgage. It might be moneylending, but there is a large difference between usury—moneylending that is oppressive, that feeds on the poor, that is wicked—and taking out a mortgage so that you can make a large purchase and spread payments out over a long period of time.

What does this mean for how we apply the Bible? It means that we need to adjust the process we go through when we seek to apply scripture to today's world. The process should be something like this:

- We have a practice today (for example, taking out mortgages).
- The Bible condemns a practice (usury).
- The practices share some similarities (both mortgages and usury involve moneylending).

Do we then condemn today's practice? It will depend. If the two are different enough, we may say, like Calvin, that the Biblical prohibitions weren't aimed at the situation we have today, even if the prohibition appears to be universal on the surface.

We are now in a position to apply this logic to the Bible and homosexuality, following the same pattern:

- In many parts of the world (Britain and the USA included) there are committed, faithful, same-sex marriages.
- The Bible condemns same-sex activity within its context.
- The two share some similarities (both involve people of the same sex).

We are left with the question: how similar are the practices condemned in the Bible to the faithful, loving, committed relationships that we are addressing today?

In the previous chapter, I outlined in general why I think the activity condemned by the Bible is vastly different from that which we are addressing in today's context. But, I understand, that is quite a big claim. If you take the Bible seriously, you will want evidence to back up this claim. In the following chapters, I address in more detail the key verses at stake, (the 'clobber' passages) which seem to condemn same-sex activity. But I shall start with some verses often used to do this, that do not address the issue directly at all. It is time to go to the beginning: Genesis.

CHAPTER 4
ADAM AND STEVE (AND EVE AND NIAMH)

'IT'S ADAM AND EVE, not Adam and Steve!'

Have you heard or read Genesis used in this way to say that homosexuality is wrong? The broader argument is that the creation accounts in Genesis only allow a man and a woman to be married. Genesis sets a pattern, or blueprint, from God for humanity, and it would be wrong to diverge from this pattern.

Let us remind ourselves of parts of the Genesis accounts:

> So God created humankind in his image, in the image of God he created them; male and female he created them. God blessed them, and God said to them, 'Be fruitful and multiply, and fill the earth...'
>
> — GENESIS 1:27-28

> Then the LORD God said, 'It is not good that the man should be alone; I will make him a helper as his partner.'
>
> Therefore a man leaves his father and his mother and clings to his wife, and they become one flesh.
>
> — GENESIS 2:18, 24

These verses paint a clear, broad picture. God creates humankind and blesses them. In particular, God blesses the union of a man and a woman.

Notice what is missing from this account. There are no clear commands or prohibitions (other than to be fruitful). We have an account, a narrative. This is the story of creation, not the creation of commands.

This leads to a key question. Are these verses *prescriptive* (it must be this way, and only this way), or are they *descriptive* (they describe what God blesses)?

I think they are descriptive. The narrative speaks to what is broadly true for most people, most of the time. Women and men fall in love, and marry, and have children, and God blesses that.

If you try to treat the accounts in Genesis as prescriptive, you quickly run into all sorts of problems.

An illustration may help. Consider the part where God says, 'be fruitful'. Is this a necessary command that must be obeyed by all? Is having children an essential element of marriage?

Many people will never be able to obey this command. For instance, some couples discover that they are unable to have children. If they discover it before the wedding, should they still marry? Or if you are already married, should you get divorced so that you can both find other people with whom to have children?

You never hear this argued in church, and you may think I'm making a petty, pedantic point. But it is not a theoretical question. Parts of ancient Judaism interpreted Genesis and other parts of the Bible in precisely this way.

Consider the following examples:

In the Mishnah (a collection of ancient Jewish oral tradition), one saying suggested that if a couple had produced no children after ten years, the husband was *obliged* to divorce his wife (*Yevamos* 64a).

Philo, a Jewish writer who lived in Egypt about the same time as Jesus, argued that marrying someone whom you knew to be infertile made you an enemy of God (Philo, *Special Laws* 3.36).

The narrative also does not address those people who would love to be married, but have yet to find the right person. Churches are full of single people. Most of them do not feel called to lifelong celibacy. Are they somehow inferior, more sinful than those who are married with children? Are they marring the image of God by being single? I suspect the majority of readers think as I do; that being married is not inherently less sinful than being single.

A small minority of people do feel called to lifelong celibacy. It is worth considering how they fit into this interpretation of Genesis. Again, this is not a purely theoretical question. Parts of ancient Judaism condemned those who voluntarily chose celibacy, declaring it contrary to God's commandments. It was the duty of every Jewish male to marry and have children.

But, for most of its history, the majority of Christianity has not interpreted Genesis in this way. The command 'be fruitful' applies, not to each individual to fulfil, but to the human race as a whole.

Too much emphasis on procreation and having children risks turning Christianity into a fertility cult.

We might also consider that being fruitful could apply to more aspects of our lives than just bearing children. For example, some people, through their service to others, are considered fruitful.

But if we are going to be prescriptive, what do we do with the later verses in Genesis? The scripture says, 'therefore a man leaves his father and mother and clings to his wife' (Gen. 2:24). In the more traditional language of the Authorised Version, the man 'cleaves unto his wife'. From this perspective, then once you are married, you should not stay at the husband's parents' house. However, many couples struggle when first married, and stay with parents to save money. A prescriptive reading of Genesis would logically imply this is sinful.

This is why it makes more sense to see Genesis as being descriptive rather than prescriptive. Yes, God blesses those who marry and move out from their parents and have children, but that does not prevent God from blessing the many others who do not fit into that particular pattern.

Once we see this, we can begin to notice other features in the account as well. Look at how the scripture says that it was not good for the human to be alone. In Genesis 2, the reason for Eve's creation is not to have children, but to be a companion. Again, not everybody finds a companion or wants one, but Eve's creation emphasises the importance of close companionship in human life, which God saw as good.

Here, we look at our world today, and see that some people find a close companion of the same sex. That bond is proclaimed in the narrative of Genesis as being a core human need.

I suppose one could argue that in Genesis the partners are male and female, not male and male or female or female. Adam and Eve, not Adam and Steve or Eve and Niamh. But this is what we should expect in a book like Genesis, which paints with a broad brush. Throughout human history, that is mostly what happens. Generally, men are attracted to women, women to men, and most couples have children.

But our situation is not about most people. We are dealing with people's stories that do not fit neatly into the main narrative, whether that is same-sex couples, those who choose celibacy, hose still looking for a partner, or those who marry but cannot have children.

This is why simply saying that Genesis is about Adam and

Eve is not a knockdown argument against homosexuality, any
more than it is a knockdown argument against being single.
God blessing Adam and Eve does not mean condemnation for
all who do not fit this pattern.

CHAPTER 5
LEVITICUS, COMMANDMENTS AND A NEW COMMANDMENT

A STUMBLING BLOCK for many Christians wanting to be more inclusive are a couple of verses in Leviticus. Do they declare homosexuality to be an abomination? And surely, if the Bible does declare homosexuality an abomination, how could it possibly be acceptable for Christians? The two verses are these:

> You shall not lie with a male as with a woman; it is an abomination.
>
> — LEVITICUS 18:22

> If a man lies with a male as with a woman, both of them have committed an abomination; they shall be put to death; their blood is upon them.
>
> — LEVITICUS 20:13

To understand these verses, we need to know a little about the background to them. We also need to consider more generally what this section of Leviticus is addressing.

Chapters 17–26 of Leviticus are sometimes called 'the holiness code'. Throughout, the section emphasises holiness; being pure. This is all encompassing. It applies to what you eat, what you do, what you are; all of these can affect how holy or ritually pure you are.

For example, eating the wrong food makes you less holy (Lev. 20:25). Leviticus categorises some food as clean, and others as unclean. Eating unclean food means 'bringing abomination' upon yourself.

Similarly, having a tattoo makes you less holy (Lev. 19:28). The same applies to wearing clothes made from a mix of fibres, for example, wool and linen (Lev. 19:19).

Even having a physical disability, according to Leviticus, will put you in this category—anyone with a disability was unable to approach the altar (Lev. 21:16–23).

What is going on here? Why is it so important not to eat certain foods, or wear mixed fibres, or have tattoos, or even to have a disability?

The holiness code is encouraging the Israelite people to be holy and pure. In particular, it encourages them to be distinct and different from their pagan worshipping neighbours. Everyday life becomes a symbol of that purity. The Israelite people are not to mix with surrounding cultures, just as different fibres are not to mix with each other in clothing.

You can see this concern about being a holy, separate people in the introduction to this section of Leviticus:

The LORD spoke to Moses, saying: Speak to the people of Israel and say to them: I am the LORD your God. You shall not do as they do in the land of Egypt, where you lived, and you shall not do as they do in the land of Canaan, to which I am bringing you. You shall not follow their statutes. My ordinances you shall observe and my statutes you shall keep, following them: I am the LORD your God. You shall keep my statutes and my ordinances; by doing so one shall live: I am the LORD.

— LEVITICUS 18:1–5

This concern also explains the prohibition of tattoos. Within the surrounding cultures, tattoos and other bodily marks were associated with ancestor worship. Israel was to be different.

How does this relate to the two verses with which we are concerned? We must consider one more aspect of the verses, which is often missed, before we can answer this question.

The verses only address males. There is no mention in the text about a woman lying with another woman. This is significant when we explore the surrounding pagan cultures.

Within these surrounding cultures, there were two socially acceptable forms of male same-sex activity.

First, male same-sex activity was associated with the act of intercourse with male shrine prostitutes as part of temple worship to a variety of pagan gods and goddesses. You can see this concern in a variety of places in the Bible:

None of the daughters of Israel shall be a temple prostitute; none of the sons of Israel shall be a temple prostitute.

— DEUT. 23:17

...there were also male temple prostitutes in the land. They committed all the abominations of the nations that the LORD drove out before the people of Israel.

— 1 KINGS 14:24

He put away the male temple prostitutes out of the land, and removed all the idols that his ancestors had made.

— 1 KINGS 15:12

He broke down the houses of the male temple prostitutes that were in the house of the LORD, where the women did weaving for Asherah.

— 2 KINGS 23:7

All of these examples show that pagan male temple prostitutes in surrounding cultures were part of the cultural background to these verses in Leviticus.

The second socially accepted form of male same-sex intercourse occurred in cultures such as ancient Greece. Here, the particular form that was prevalent was men (usually married) with boys: pederasty. I have already explained some of this background in chapter two, which focused particularly on the New Testament period. However, the same was broadly true in earlier centuries. Ancient Greece had some differences: the boys involved would usually be free rather than enslaved, but at its root it was the same phenomenon.

This second reason might be why the two key verses specify a man lying with a *male*, not a man lying with a man. The word 'male' is deliberately chosen to target pederasty in the prohibition.

Some commentators claim that male is specified because of a link to Genesis 1:27, 'male and female he created them'. However, if this is meant to be a reference, it is strange that 'female' is not used in the verses anywhere. The reference is 'as with a woman', not with a 'female'. There is also no reference at all to female same-sex activity. For these reasons, I think that it is more likely that 'male' is used precisely because it encompasses men lying with boys.

Therefore, there are two main cultural contexts from which the people of Israel are called to be different: male-male intercourse associated with pagan worship; and pederasty.

If, therefore, we are meant to take these two verses from Leviticus seriously as a rule for Christian life, we ought to take into account the context and purpose for these verses, which is different from our context today.

There is, though, a weightier issue in interpreting how to apply these verses today. Should Christians even be attempting to obey these verses strictly and literally, on the basis that they are in the Bible?

Most of us are not even consistent in how we might obey these particular verses. Leviticus 20:13 specifies execution for transgression: 'they shall be put to death'. Unless you are willing to argue that homosexuality deserves the death penalty, then you are contextualising the second part of the verse. Even if you might decide that homosexuality deserves capital punishment (and I sincerely hope that you do not), are you prepared to be consistent, and also demand the death penalty for adultery (consider Leviticus 20:10)?

We can also return to the issue of tattoos. According to Leviticus, anyone with a tattoo should cut off from the community. Or perhaps we can consider the perils of the wardrobe: do you buy clothes with a mix of fibres?

Perhaps we should return to the issue of clean and unclean food. If you are not a vegetarian, do you ever have a ham and cheese sandwich? Do you ever eat bacon or pork? All of these foods are, according to Leviticus, unclean, and eating any of it is bringing abomination upon yourself.

Looking more broadly, many Christians are content with breaking one of the Ten Commandments on a regular basis.

They work on a Saturday, and Saturday (more precisely, sundown on Friday until sundown on Saturday) is the Sabbath.

Some Christians might claim that they keep Sunday as a special day. However, there is absolutely nothing in the Old Testament about keeping Sunday, the first day of the week, as special in any way. That does not mean that keeping Sunday as a day of rest is wrong, but it does mean that the Old Testament law has been altered and reinterpreted for a different context.

Most Christians do not worry about these issues, and the reason for this goes back to the first debate in the church. This was about whether non-Jewish (Gentile) Christians had to keep the Law, the Torah, of which Leviticus is a part. This debate is the background to some of Paul's letters (particularly Galatians and Romans), and parts of the Acts of the Apostles (particularly Acts 10–15).

The outcome of this dispute was that Gentiles did not have to keep the Jewish Torah. Paul's letters give some of the theological background to the reason for this. With the arrival of the Messiah, Jesus, the time of the Law, the Torah, has come to an end:

> For Christ is the end of the law so that there may be right-eousness for everyone who believes.
>
> — ROMANS 10:4

> Now before faith came, we were imprisoned and guarded under the law until faith would be revealed. Therefore the law was our disciplinarian until Christ came, so that we might be justified by faith. But now that faith has come, we are no longer subject to a disciplinarian, for in Christ Jesus you are all children of God through faith.
>
> — GALATIANS 3:23–26

The Law has been fulfilled in Christ, and in its place we have been given a new law—the law of love. Paul the apostle expresses it in this way:

> For the whole law is summed up in a single commandment, "You shall love your neighbour as yourself."
>
> — GALATIANS 5:14

This is why Christians can get a tattoo, wear a cotton-polyester blend shirt, enjoy a bacon sandwich, or take a job that includes work on Saturdays. The only consideration is whether what you are doing is loving. Of course, there is going to be much overlap with the Torah. To take two of the Ten Commandments, it is not loving to bear false witness, or to steal, (except in extremely unusual circumstances) for example. However, the overriding consideration should not be whether a command is in Leviticus or any of the other books of the Torah, but whether our actions demonstrate love to our neighbours.

Despite this clear approach outlined by the New Testament, I have sometimes been asked whether it applies to the two verses in question. Leviticus 18:22 and 20:13 both deal with sexual morality. Surely sexual morality does not change? Therefore here, so it is argued, we should follow Leviticus.

However, just three verses away from Leviticus 18:22, we find this verse about sexual morality:

> You shall not approach a woman to uncover her nakedness while she is in her menstrual uncleanness.
>
> — LEVITICUS 18:19

To put this more directly, Leviticus commands no intercourse while a woman has her period. It is in the same section as one of the verses we are considering; Leviticus considers it just as bad, just as much of an abomination, as a man lying with a male.

Despite this command in Leviticus, I have never heard any warnings about not having intercourse during a period in sermons. I have never read this as something for Christians to consider seriously in any Christian book. It is not mentioned, to the best of my knowledge, in any Christian marriage preparation course.

The only time I have seen it considered is recently in a non-affirming evangelical podcast, in response to a listener question. The podcast advised that this law no longer applied absolutely to Christians; couples could decide at their own discretion.

Why is this verse not generally mentioned or preached on? Because we do not consider it to apply to us. The time of the Law has come to an end, and the only law for Christians to follow is the law of love.

A short summary may be helpful. There are a variety of possible contexts for the verses in Leviticus, but two prominent ones are intercourse with male shrine prostitutes at temples to pagan goddesses, and intercourse between married men and boys. Neither is similar to the context we are considering today.

However, in any case, we do not look to Leviticus for rules to run our lives. Christ has given us the only rule we need: love one another.

If I am honest, I do not understand the constant appeals to Leviticus, plucking these two verses out and ignoring the other commands in that book.

The verses in Leviticus do not mean that the Bible forbids same-sex relationships in today's different context.

One rejoinder is that perhaps the verses in Leviticus on their own do not carry enough weight, but the Bible also contains a narrative about the evil of homosexuality, resulting in the destruction of whole cities, so wicked does God consider it. This is the story of Sodom and Gomorrah. As you might expect, there is an alternative perspective on this account, which I will consider in the next chapter.

CHAPTER 6
THE SIN OF SODOM

THE CHANCES ARE, if you are reading this book, that you have been told at some point that the sin of Sodom was homosexuality. We even name male-male intercourse 'sodomy' from this account.

But the sin of Sodom was not homosexuality, and in this chapter I shall explain why. First, a quick recap of what happens in the narrative; the full version can be found in Genesis 18–19.

God sends two angels to the city of Sodom, known for its wickedness. Lot, Abraham's nephew, lives there. Lot welcomes the angels and offers them hospitality, persuading them to stay the night. They accept, and he lays on a lavish feast for them.

However, word gets out, and all the men of the town surround the house. They demand that the visitor be brought out so that they can rape them (many Biblical versions translate the Hebrew literally, 'so that we may know them', but most commentators agree that this is a euphemism for sexual intercourse). Lot tries to protect his visitors, even offering his own daughters in their place (this is problematic for a whole range of new reasons). The mob rejects Lot's offer, and in a fury try to attack.

The angels blind the mob and drag Lot and his family away from the city. God destroys the cities of Sodom and Gomorrah by fire. Lot's wife looks back, and is turned into a pillar of salt. Only Lot and his daughters escape with their lives.

It is a dramatic account, and no wonder that Sodom becomes a by-word for an evil city. However, consider how the rest of the Bible remembers Sodom and its misdeeds.

Isaiah, in condemnatory mode, compares the nation of Judah to Sodom and Gomorrah, saying that Judah needs to learn to do good, to seek justice, to rescue the oppressed, to defend the orphan, and to plead for the widow (Isaiah 1:9–17). There is no mention of sexual sin.

The same pattern holds later in Isaiah, where Judah is judged for being like Sodom. Why? Because the people are 'grinding the faces of the poor' (Isaiah 3:15).

Another prophet, Ezekiel, comments:

> This was the guilt of your sister Sodom: she and her daughters had pride, excess of food, and prosperous ease, but did not aid the poor and needy. They were haughty, and did abominable things before me; therefore I removed them when I saw it.

> — EZEKIEL 16:49–50

In other parts of the Bible, it is the fate of Sodom which is emphasised. The message is: watch out, or you will end up worse than Sodom and Gomorrah.

What we find, therefore, is a range of accusations that focus upon injustice, oppression of the poor and doing abominable things.

With this in mind, let us return to the account. At the heart of the narrative is a grotesque, evil act: an attempted gang rape by an enraged mob. One could rightly call it abominable.

Clearly, the male mob wished to rape visitors whom they perceived as men. However, rape is not about sex or gender. Rape is about power, and control, and humiliation.

In Britain, TV celebrity Jimmy Savile left a trail of both male and female survivors of his abuse. He was unconcerned with gender; opportunity and power were the driving factors.

After the Iraq war, the Abu Ghraib prison became notorious for the assaults and rapes inflicted upon both female and male prisoners. Again, the gender of the prisoners was immaterial. The concern was humiliation.

The Sodom account is an attempted gang rape. What has this to do with committed, loving relationships? And, in particular, what has it got to do with the gender of those involved?

The irrelevance of gender in this account is shown by a similar account in Judges 19. A short recap follows:

A man and his female concubine enter a city and are offered hospitality. The men of the city come at night demanding that this visitor be thrown out to them to be raped. The concubine is offered to the mob in place of the man. She is raped and killed, left for dead on the doorstep to be found in the morning. The mob did not care about the gender of their victim.

Same-sex rape or heterosexual rape, rape is rape. It is about violence, having little to do with gender, and nothing to do with any kind of loving relationship.

Of all the verses commonly quoted as proof that the Bible is against homosexuality, the account in Sodom is the least relevant. It has nothing to offer us as we consider how we interpret the Bible in the context of loving same-sex relationships.

CHAPTER 7

THE SILENCE OF THE GOSPELS

THE GOSPELS SAY nothing directly about homosexuality.

This should not come as a surprise; I have already explained how nothing in the Bible is directly about homosexuality. We can go further, though. Not only is there nothing directly about homosexuality, there is also nothing directly in the gospels about same-sex activity.

This has not stopped many people (on both sides of the argument) from claiming that it does, or appealing to parts of the gospel to shore up their arguments.

I should be clear: I am not saying that the gospels are irrelevant to the debates around sexuality and gender. Indirectly, there is much from which to learn. I am saying that I often see the gospels misused in these issues.

Let me give you an example.

One strategy in the arguments is to appeal to what Jesus would have said or done, had he been confronted with the issue. This is a forceful approach; who are we to disagree with Jesus?

Those on the affirming side sometimes say that Jesus accepted everybody, including those treated as outcasts by others. Therefore, Jesus accepts people who are LGBTQI+. The argument contains an important truth; Jesus did accept people marginalised by others, such as tax-collectors and prostitutes.

However, the counter-argument that someone who is non-affirming may produce is that Jesus also told people to stop sinning. If it is sinful to have intercourse with someone of the same gender as yourself, then Jesus would presumably also say 'stop sinning' about this issue.

The disagreement comes because both sides are working from different assumptions; the affirming side does not believe same-sex intercourse is sinful; the non-affirming side does. The appeal to Jesus is therefore unconvincing to the non-affirming side.

We also see the same difficulties with arguments produced by those on the non-affirming side. For example, they will argue that Jesus was a first century Jewish man, and must be understood within the first century Jewish context. Any first century Jewish man, they argue, would condemn same-sex intercourse. Therefore, Jesus would condemn same-sex intercourse.

Again, this argument contains an important truth. It is vital to recognise the Jewish context of Jesus. However, it also omits an even more important truth: for Christians, Jesus is not just *any* first century Jewish man; he is also God. You cannot therefore simply assume that Jesus will react the same way as the culture at the time. To do so is to limit God to first century culture.

Another approach used by both sides is the argument from silence. Those on the affirming side might argue, 'Jesus said nothing against homosexuality. As he did not condemn it, it must be OK'. The difficulty with this argument is that there are many practices that Jesus never explicitly condemned, but that does not mean that they are fine. For example, Jesus never explicitly condemned slavery.

The counter-argument from silence runs like this, 'the

reason Jesus said nothing is that it would have been so obvious to all around that it was wrong that it did not need saying'. However, this is also pure speculation.

We are in danger of filling the silence by voicing our own presuppositions.

Some arguments (again, on both sides) go beyond the silence of Jesus and look to his words or actions. These need deeper unpacking. You may come across three particular passages used in these arguments:

- Jesus talks about marriage (Matthew 19:3–12; see also Mark 10:2–12);
- Jesus talks about sexual immorality (Mark 7:17–23);
- Jesus heals a centurion's slave (Luke 7:1–10).

Let us look first at the passage where Jesus talks about marriage. Some pharisees come to test Jesus, and ask him how easy he thinks it should be for a husband to divorce his wife.

This was a current debate in the Judaism of the time.

One school of thought, following a Jewish teacher called Hillel, argued that a husband should be able to divorce his wife for any reason at all. For example, a husband would have grounds for divorcing his wife if she burned his meal while cooking it.

Another school of thought was stricter, and generally followed a Jewish teacher called Shammai. This school held that the only grounds for divorce was if the wife committed adultery.

According to Matthew's account, Jesus aligns himself with this stricter school. A husband could not abandon his wife just for trivial reasons, but only for infidelity.

The reason that Jesus gives goes back to the creation account of Genesis:

He answered, "Have you not read that the one who made them at the beginning 'made them male and female,' and said, 'For this reason a man shall leave his father and mother and be joined to his wife, and the two shall become one flesh'? So they are no longer two, but one flesh. Therefore what God has joined together, let no one separate."

— MATTHEW 19:4–6

Let us be clear about the issue at stake here. Jesus is addressing the *permanence* of marriage, and not *who* you can marry. Jesus is not being asked about whether only men and women can get married.

Jesus' response, therefore, addresses whether marriage should be life-long, and not whether same-sex relationships and marriages can be honouring to God. Jesus strongly affirms traditional marriage, but he does not, by doing this, condemn all alternatives.

It might be thought that I am being unfair to the argument here. Jesus does not just affirm traditional marriage; he also links it directly to God's plans in creation. If this is God's plan for humanity, then surely, the argument goes, we should take this seriously.

This is true, to a point. Jesus does affirm the Genesis account, that God blesses the union of men and women. However, that does not mean that alternatives are condemned by God. The arguments presented in the chapter on Genesis apply here. As an example, celibacy is not part of the pattern presented in Genesis, yet most Christians would not argue that it was therefore condemned.

Just as the passage is silent about celibacy, it is also silent about same-sex relationships. Any attempts to make it speak to this issue are arguments based on speculation.

We can reflect further on these verses. Many protestant

traditions, including evangelical ones, hold that, in certain circumstances, remarriage after divorce is possible. This comes from nuanced reflection on this passage, and other passages on marriage in the New and Old Testaments.

But you can't go from nuanced interpretations about the permanence of marriage, which Jesus addresses directly, and then use the same passage as a blunt instrument to condemn same-sex relationships, about which the passage is silent. To use the passage in that way would smack of double standards.

The second passage comes from Mark 7. Jesus proclaims that it is not what enters our bodies physically that defiles us, but what comes out from our hearts:

> It is what comes out of a person that defiles. For it is from within, from the human heart, that evil intentions come: fornication, theft, murder, adultery, avarice, wickedness, deceit, licentiousness, envy, slander, pride, folly. All these evil things come from within, and they defile a person.

> — MARK 7:20

The debate here centres around the word translated as 'fornication'. The original Greek word in the New Testament is *porneiai*. Another way of translating it would be 'sexual immoralities' (the word is plural). This Greek word is the root of some English words like 'pornography'.

Some people have argued that this plural form of sexual immoralities would immediately lead any first century Israelite to think of the list of forbidden offences in Leviticus 18 and 20. These offences include incest, bestiality, adultery, and also male same-sex intercourse.

The argument is wrong, for a number of reasons. First, there is no particular significance in this word being plural. All the sins mentioned by Jesus in this passage are plural. A more literal translation would say, 'sexual immoralities, murders, adulteries...' and so forth. This makes sense, because Jesus is addressing the evil intentions (plural) that come from the heart. 'Sexual immoralities' is therefore of no particular significance as pointing to parts of Leviticus.

Secondly, the argument also misunderstands how *porneia* (that is the singular form, so 'sexual immorality') was understood within that context.

The original root of *porneia* comes from words associated with prostitution. It gradually expanded in scope to include sleeping around more generally. Within Judaism, it also became associated with idolatry, partly through the use of the metaphor of Israel being unfaithful to God, though it is less likely that that is what Jesus or his listeners would have had in mind here.

You might also notice what at first could seem puzzling. Jesus refers both to sexual immorality and also to adultery. Why would someone include both? Is adultery not a type of sexual immorality?

The apparent duplication is because Roman law defined adultery narrowly. Adultery only referred to sleeping with a free man's wife or daughter. Intercourse with prostitutes or those who were enslaved was not, legally speaking, adultery.

We can now make more sense of what Jesus was saying. Evil intentions include sexual immoralities, which is sleeping around generally (for example with prostitutes or those enslaved), and also adultery, which is sleeping with other free people's wives or daughters.

These two occur together in a number of places in the New Testament (1 Cor. 6:9, Heb. 13:4) and in early Christian writings. The reference is therefore not to specific offences in Leviticus, but to a much more general condemnation of sexual immorality.

The third reason the argument is wrong is that this is not

how rabbis commonly used the term. For example, in talking about the offences in Leviticus, the rabbis did not generally use *porneia* (in either its singular or plural form) or its Hebrew equivalent. In fact, they specifically designated some of the offences in this section of Leviticus as not being *porneia*.

These three reasons demonstrate that Jesus was referring more widely to sexual immorality, and not specifically to a group of commandments in Leviticus 18 and 20.

When looking with others at what the gospels say, I sometimes get the response, 'yes, but Jesus does say sexual immorality is wrong, and that includes any sexual activity outside marriage'. Jesus may not have specifically singled out same-sex activity, but it is included in the more general condemnation, they argue.

At first sight, this looks convincing. However, the argument only works if you consider same-sex activity and same-sex marriage to be sinful in the first place. If same-sex activity is not intrinsically sinful, then it is not intrinsically a form of sexual immorality.

Whether or not same-sex activity is always sinful is what we are trying to determine; arguments that begin with that assumption that to start with are not valid.

We should also look back at the context in Mark to see how it goes against the grain of how the gospel depicts Jesus' teaching.

The issue in Mark 7 is about what defiles a person. Jesus' disciples are in trouble because they were seen eating without washing their hands (the importance here relates to ritual washing—this is not about hygiene).

Jesus responds by saying that his critics are emphasising adherence to rules rather than the original intent behind the rule.

In particular, he argues that it is not the physical that makes us impure. What enters our bodies from outside cannot render us unclean. What matters is what is in our hearts.

The immediate issue in the account in Mark is about food, but the broader issue is relevant here as well. Assuming that same-sex activity is intrinsically sinful is analogous to saying that some foods are intrinsically sinful to eat.

Jesus declared all foods clean; what matters is whether our hearts are evil. We can apply the same principle to issues of sexuality.

The third passage used in arguments about the gospels and sexuality is the account in Luke of Jesus healing the centurion's slave. Here is the beginning of the account:

> A centurion there had a slave whom he valued highly, and who was ill and close to death. When he heard about Jesus, he sent some Jewish elders to him, asking him to come and heal his slave. When they came to Jesus, they appealed to him earnestly, saying, "He is worthy of having you do this for him, for he loves our people, and it is he who built our synagogue for us." And Jesus went with them, but when he was not far from the house, the centurion sent friends to say to him, "Lord, do not trouble yourself, for I am not worthy to have you come under my roof; therefore I did not presume to come to you. But only speak the word, and let my servant [*pais*] be healed. For I also am a man set under authority, with soldiers under me; and I say to one, 'Go,' and he goes, and to another, 'Come,' and he comes, and to my slave, 'Do this,' and the slave does it." When Jesus heard this he was amazed at him, and turning to the crowd that followed him, he said, "I tell you, not even in Israel have I found such faith." When those who had been sent returned to the house, they found the slave in good health.
>
> — LUKE 7:2–7

You may be wondering why this passage is relevant at all. On the face of it, Jesus performs a miraculous healing at a distance for a centurion with great faith. What has this to do with arguments over sexuality?

The reason the passage comes up is because this passage is sometimes presented as Jesus healing a gay centurion's lover.

I am first going to show why people argue this, and then go on to explain why I do not think this passage should be used.

The background to this is that Roman soldiers were not allowed to marry whilst on active service; they had to wait until they retired. It was not uncommon for senior military officers (like a centurion) to have enslaved people, including boys. And, sadly, it was not uncommon for the officers to use these enslaved boys for intercourse.

The centurion in Luke's account says, 'only speak the word, and let my servant be healed'. The word translated as servant here is *pais*. It can have multiple meanings. The word usually means child, or given that the enslaved person was male (we know that from the word for enslaved person used earlier in the passage), 'boy'. However, 'boy' could also be used as a term for any enslaved male.

Was this a gay centurion asking for healing for his lover? And does Jesus praising the centurion mean that he accepted gay relationships?

That is reading too much into the passage in a number of ways.

First, it is historically plausible that this centurion was using his slave for intercourse. However, it is also plausible that he was not. Luke simply does not give enough information for us to be able to tell one way or the other.

Secondly, even if the centurion was using his slave, that does not mean that the centurion was gay, as we understand the term. As explained in chapter two, the ancient world did not categorise sexuality by the gender of your partner, but by whether you were the active, dominant partner or the submissive, passive partner.

Of those centurions who did use their slaves for intercourse, many would have gone on to marry women upon retirement. The ancient Roman world would have seen this as perfectly acceptable and normal.

If we apply our understanding of sexuality onto relationships in the ancient world, we are in danger of going wrong. We have absolutely no idea whether or not the centurion was gay, and it would not have been a question that the Roman world would have thought to ask.

Thirdly, the silence of Jesus cannot be taken to imply his consent to such a relationship. Following this logic, we might also infer that Jesus not only approved of the centurion's relationship with his slave, but also the institution of slavery itself.

If you think this is far-fetched, pro-slavery evangelical scholars in the eighteenth and nineteenth century used the silence of Jesus over slavery as part of their arguments. Few of us now would think these arguments hold water.

Fourthly, and most importantly, this is not a relationship to which I would want to appeal. It is not consensual; it is master–enslaved person. Such relationships are inherently abusive.

Therefore, if the centurion was in a relationship with his slave, it is utterly different to the type of relationships that we are considering today: committed, faithful, loving, consensual relationships.

Trying to use the account of the healing of the centurion's slave is, in my view, a misstep.

To summarise this chapter: both sides appeal to different passages in the gospels to support their positions. However, both sides try to build fortresses on a foundation of sand. Arguments that gospel passages directly address the issue of sexuality fall short when examined closely.

The gospels say nothing directly about homosexuality.

CHAPTER 8
READING ROMANS THE RIGHT WAY

DOES Paul clearly and explicitly condemn all homosexual practice in his letter to the Romans? Because so many people assume that this is the case, the verses in Romans 1 are probably the most important in the entire Bible for our issue. But, I do not think Paul does condemn homosexuality, and in this chapter, I will lay out my reasons, so you can decide for yourself.

I shall first lay out the cultural context, in particular around sexuality, in which Romans was written, a context far different from our own. Secondly, I shall outline Paul's argument in Romans 1. Thirdly, I shall show the different possibilities of what Paul meant by 'against nature' in Romans 1:26. Fourthly, I shall look at various understandings of the background to 'males in males' in Romans 1:27. Putting these aspects together, I shall demonstrate why I think it is a mistake to think that Paul is condemning homosexuality here.

People often claim that the plain meaning of Romans clearly condemns both lesbianism and homosexuality. If you take the Word of God seriously, they will say, you need to take Paul's condemnation seriously.

However, the people in the churches to which Paul was

writing might have thought that the plain meaning of Romans was something entirely different.

'The past is a foreign country: they do things differently there.' The first line of L.P. Hartley's *The Go-Between* is as true for Roman times as it is for that book's setting at the birth of the twentieth century. To understand Paul's letter, we need to understand Paul's world and how foreign some elements might seem to us.

To begin, we need to recap some of the features of that time which were outlined in chapter two. The ancient Roman world saw sexuality differently from the current Western world. There were no categories of 'heterosexual' or 'homosexual' as specific, separate orientations. We can find occasional comments about certain people who seemed to favour inter-course only with their own gender, but these are rare.

The main categories for sexuality revolved around practice: who was the dominant, active, penetrating partner in an encounter; and who was the submissive, passive, penetrated partner. What mattered were your status and power, not your gender.

For a freeborn man to maintain his high status and honour, he would have to act as the dominant, active partner in any encounter. In contrast, a woman, who had lower status in that society, was expected to be the submissive, passive partner. This basic pattern carried into a wide range of sexual encounters. For example, a freeborn male could also have intercourse with:

- boys (roughly speaking, from age ten until when a beard first started to appear);
- enslaved people of either sex (they had no honour and no rights);
- prostitutes whether male or female (because prostitutes had no honour); and

- actors or bar staff (because they too, legally, had no honour within that culture).

There were some differences amongst cultures of the time; within Roman culture freeborn boys were out of bounds, whereas within Greek culture it was more acceptable for freeborn boys to be used.

Sleeping with someone else's freeborn wife or daughter was not acceptable, because that violated honour.

Since enslaved people and prostitutes had no honour to violate, intercourse with people in either category was not adultery. And Roman society provided many such opportunities. Let me give you an example.

Some years ago, I was able to explore the ancient ruins of Ephesus (if you get the opportunity, take it: these are second only to Pompeii in what was been preserved). A highlight is the magnificent façade of the library; two stories of marble rising high above you, adorned with numerous Corinthian style columns. Our guide recounted how magnificent the library was in its heyday (it was built in the early second century). Then, he also pointed out that there was a tunnel leading from the library directly to the main brothel.

A married man might leave for the library, have intercourse with a prostitute, return home and retire for the night with his wife. In doing all of this, he would not have incurred any particular shame or notoriety. It was just part of the social landscape.

So pervasive was this attitude that in the first few centuries church leaders had a difficult time persuading their congregations that intercourse with prostitutes was wrong. Men in the church argued back that it was both legal and provided a natural outlet for sexual urges.

Salvian, a fifth century bishop, described Roman attitudes here in just four words: 'forbidding adulteries, building brothels'.

It was not just prostitutes who were used by men, it was also those they had enslaved.

Sometimes, I come across Christians who have been told that slavery in Roman times was not too bad. It was different, they are informed, from the antebellum American South. Roman masters cared for and provided for those they enslaved, and considered them part of the family.

This is nonsense.

Slavery, whether ancient or more recent, is wicked. Let me show you some reasons why slavery in the time of the Roman empire was cruel and unjust.

Imagine that you are an enslaved person in the time of the New Testament, working in the household of a wealthy citizen.

You are his property. He owns you, just as nowadays we might own cars or dishwashers. (The car analogy might be particularly appropriate; many people could not afford one, some households might have one or two, whereas rich people might have many.) He can use you as he sees fit. He has power of life and death over you.

You bring him some food. He considers it slightly too hot, or cold, and has you whipped.

You wish to marry another enslaved person in the household, but enslaved persons are not legally allowed to marry. You privately pledge to each other, live as if you were legally married, and have a child together. The child now also belongs to your master. One day, your master decides to sell your partner and child, and you never see either of them again.

Your master decides he has sexual urges that need fulfilling. You are to hand; he decides to use you. There is no issue of consent, because you are his property.

If you try to fight back, or rebel against him, he can decide to have you killed.

There was a standard, common way to deal with enslaved people who rebelled against their masters: crucifixion.

Masters used and abused those they enslaved as they saw fit. And, as was said in a previous chapter, there were even specific terms (*deliciae* and *concubinus*) for enslaved boys that were to be used sexually.

This was the Roman world to which Paul was writing.

But Paul was Jewish.

What were Jewish attitudes to intercourse? The Judaism of the time strongly linked prostitution and idolatry, and condemned both. Similarly, pederasty was also linked with idolatry, and was condemned.

But many strands of Judaism at the time also condemned any type of intercourse that was non-procreative—that is, any type of intercourse that could not result in a pregnancy.

This was a contrast to the Graeco-Roman world at that time, which generally accepted practices such as anal intercourse, in part because this was a method of birth control.

Early Christianity shared some attitudes with Judaism, which is unsurprising as Christianity was Jewish at its start.

For example, an early Christian teaching manual says:

> You shall not murder; you shall not commit adultery; you shall not corrupt children; you shall not be sexually immoral...
>
> — *DIDACHE* 2:2

As we have seen before, adultery is listed separately from sexual immorality, and child corruption (which is referring to pederasty) is listed separately again.

Of these three, only adultery would be widely condemned by all three cultures: Jewish, Christian and Graeco-Roman.

You may be wondering how people then reacted to women having sex with women. The ancient world, at least in official, written sources, was not terribly interested.

In part, that was because 'intercourse' was not seen as really taking place. There was no penetration, and no possibility of children.

Additionally, this was a male-dominated society, where in general women were less important. Therefore, what women did together was seen as not particularly significant.

This is not to say that female-female sex did not take place. We know that it did. But the evidence comes mostly from unofficial, private sources. We have written spells, dream interpretations and other evidence that has only relatively recently been compiled and studied.

The Graeco-Roman world, therefore, looked down on women having intercourse with women, but did not usually refer to it.

The Jewish cultures of the time were similar. If anything, the evidence points to female-female sexual intercourse being treated less seriously in Judaism.

In part, that is because it is not forbidden in the Torah, and in part because no penetration was involved. Some rabbis treated it as being a similar offence to masturbation.

There were debates about whether females who engaged in same-sex activity were eligible to marry priests or not. The lack of importance given to the practice demonstrates how it was not treated as being serious, and also how it was treated differently from male same-sex activity.

Of particular importance for our understanding, female-female intercourse was not seen as being parallel to male-male intercourse, but as belonging to a completely different category.

I have begun with this broad sweep looking at attitudes to sexuality in the first century because understanding this background is crucial in interpreting Romans. We can now turn to what Paul wrote to the churches in Rome.

My focus is going to be mainly on Romans 1. However, we

also need to delve into Romans 2 as well, as this enables us to understand better what Paul is trying to achieve in Romans 1.

Paul's overall purpose is to explain the gospel; the good news that Jesus died on the cross for us. He comes to that in Romans 3:21f. Before that, he outlines the problem for humankind.

We need to notice something else going on. Paul, throughout Romans, addresses two groups of people: Jewish people and Gentiles (often using the word 'Greek' to represent Gentiles). It is a repeated motif:

> For I am not ashamed of the gospel; it is the power of God for salvation to everyone who has faith, to the Jew first and also to the Greek.
>
> — ROMANS 1:16

> There will be anguish and distress for everyone who does evil, the Jew first and also the Greek, but glory and honour and peace for everyone who does good, the Jew first and also the Greek.
>
> — ROMANS 2:9–10

> What then? Are we any better off? No, not at all; for we have already charged that all, both Jews and Greeks, are under the power of sin...
>
> — ROMANS 3:9

> Or is God the God of Jews only? Is he not the God of Gentiles also? Yes, of Gentiles also...
>
> — ROMANS 3:29

...including us whom he has called, not from the Jews only but also from the Gentiles?

— ROMANS 9:24

For there is no distinction between Jew and Greek; the same Lord is Lord of all and is generous to all who call on him.

— ROMANS 10:12

Paul is keen to emphasise that, whether or not you are Jewish or Gentile, everyone is in the same need of Christ and, whether you are Jewish or Gentile, all who put their trust in Christ will be saved.

Most scholars believe that Paul is addressing tensions between different church congregations in Rome, where some were mostly Jewish Christians and others mostly Gentile Christians.

In Romans 1, he begins to lay out the need that Gentiles have for Christ. He does so by using a form of attack that would be familiar with many Jewish listeners; it is a stereotypical Jewish diatribe against Gentile society (you can see a similar example in the Wisdom of Solomon 13–14).

This attack is also, according to the majority of commentators, a sting operation against the Jewish listener. The Gentiles, the pagans, worship created things rather than the creator; in other words, they turned to idolatry.

The results of idolatry are awful, and evil, and God judges them. The Jewish listener is expected to be nodding along, only to be caught out in chapter 2 where Paul effectively tells them, 'you're no better than the pagans'.

The diatribe begins with Paul describing the replacement of worship of God with images of humans, or birds, or beasts, or reptiles:

Claiming to be wise, they became fools; and they exchanged
the glory of the immortal God for images resembling a mortal
human being or birds or four-footed animals or reptiles.

— ROMANS 1:22–23

Some have seen echoes of Genesis 1 in this passage. It is
difficult to be sure, though it would make some sense given the
contrast between creator and created.

However, the passage is not describing the fall. The critique
is not aimed at all humankind, but is focused on pagans. The
charge is not that they disobeyed God (the sin of Adam and
Eve), but that they turned from worship of God to idols.

The consequences of this idolatry are that God gives them
up, a phrase that Paul repeats three times:

Therefore God gave them up in the lusts of their hearts to
impurity, to the degrading of their bodies among
themselves...

— ROMANS 1:24

For this reason God gave them up to degrading passions.

— ROMANS 1:26

God gave them up to a debased mind and to things that
should not be done.

— ROMANS 1:28

Many have seen God's punishment as allowing events to
take their course; if you turn from worshipping God, God lets
you suffer the consequences.

With this overall structure in mind (an attack on pagan idolatry leading to dire consequences), we can now turn to the key verses. Here, rather than rely on published versions of the Bible, I am going to provide my own translation, as other versions obscure important details:

> On account of this [the Gentile idolatry] God handed them over to dishonourable passions: for both their females exchanged the natural usage for the usage against nature, likewise also the males, having left the natural usage of females, were burnt up in their desire for each other, males in males doing that which brought shame and receiving in themselves the due rewards which inevitably came from their going astray.
>
> — ROMANS 1:26–27

There are a number of features that need our attention in this passage. In particular, I am going to focus on the following: what Paul might mean by 'against nature'; what females 'exchanging the natural usage' might refer to; and why Paul writes about 'males in males'.

'Against nature' (*para physin*) could have a variety of meanings.

Within Paul's own writings, 'nature' elsewhere seems to refer broadly to the natural order of things. Going against it can be negative, such as long hair on a man (1 Corinthians 11:14), but it can also be positive, such as God grafting Gentiles into the 'olive tree' of Judaism (Romans 11:24).

For other Jewish writers of the time, such as Philo, 'against nature' could mean any type of intercourse that couldn't lead to a pregnancy. Under this heading would come a variety of practices, such as oral and anal intercourse, intercourse during menstruation, using any form of contraception, and also having intercourse if it was known that one of the partners was infertile (Philo allows intercourse if the man married the woman not knowing of infertility, but would prohibit a marriage where this was known beforehand).

This leads to our first issue in applying these verses. If we were to stick with one common Jewish understanding as to what was 'against nature' at the time, it would rule out contraception, marriage between older couples beyond child-bearing age, and marriage where one of the partners is infertile.

Most traditions and denominations in the protestant tradition would not hold to these prohibitions.

It is also possible that Paul was using the term in a different way. Within the wider Graeco-Roman world, 'against nature' could also be a way of referring to excessive, uncontrolled sexual desire, which went beyond normal bounds.

Self-control was a key virtue in this world. If Paul meant this, then he was condemning excessive, uncontrolled lust. He was not condemning same-sex attraction as a separate category of desire, as the Graeco-Roman world did not categorise sexuality as being heterosexual versus homosexual. Rather, it was a demonstration of desire beyond bounds. This understanding of Paul has been heavily championed by some scholars.

For completeness, I should also mention that going against or beyond nature could just refer to something unexpected. For example, an enslaved person being loyal to a master to the point of death is described in Appian, *Civil Wars* 4.38 as going 'beyond nature' (*hyper physin*).

Gender also played a part in how the Graeco-Roman world understood sexuality, but in a way that is unfamiliar to many in the modern world. Excessive, uncontrolled lust was seen as a feminine trait. To be masculine was to be self-controlled, while weaker women, so the stereotype held, were less controlled.

A summary may help: 'against nature' could have a variety of meanings, but in all cases it seems to refer to something going beyond the natural order of things (where the 'natural order' depended upon the worldview at the time).

Having looked at the phrase 'against nature', we can now consider what Paul could have meant by 'exchanging the natural usage'. Did Paul have female-female sex in mind?

You may think that the answer is obviously yes. But look carefully at what Paul says, and does not say; he does not explicitly indicate that two women are involved, that this is lesbian activity.

In favour of the view that Paul did mean female-female sex is the parallel with the following verse, where he is explicit that male-male intercourse is meant. However, there are also serious problems with this interpretation. Below are some of the issues.

First, why would Paul raise female-female sex first? In the ancient world, dominated by men, and where men get talked or written about first, this is surprising.

Commentators on this passage sometimes skirt around this inconvenient feature, and try to find a reason for it. Some suggest it demonstrates Paul's egalitarianism by talking about women first. Others suggest that Paul is starting with the worst example.

These attempts generally ignore how odd it would be for Paul to be writing about female-female sex at all. There are few references to it in Jewish writings of the period, and not many more in the formal writings of the wider Graeco-Roman world.

Additionally, as we have already seen, Jewish writings did not consider female-female sex to be particularly awful, nor as being a parallel or equivalent to intercourse where penetration by a male was involved.

To add to the issues, the logic of the rhetoric means that Paul should be raising a practice tolerated by Gentiles but condemned by Jewish people of the time. Female-female intercourse does not fit this logic: Jewish people did not particularly condemn it, and the wider Gentile world looked down on it. In other words, lesbianism was not seen as a specifically Gentile vice.

There is one other factor when considering whether Paul was referring to female-female sex; how the early church interpreted this passage. They did not understand Paul to be referring to female-female sex here until the late fourth century, and even then there was variety in how the passage was understood.

Is there an alternative understanding? Yes. As outlined above, in Jewish sources 'unnatural usage' could be any type of intercourse which could not result in a pregnancy. In wider sources, 'unnatural usage' could mean excessive, uncontrolled sex.

This means that females exchanging 'the natural usage for the usage against nature' could refer to women engaging in forms of intercourse with men, such as anal intercourse (perhaps used as a method of contraception), which were widely accepted in Gentile society, but not within Judaism.

In other words, in Romans 1 Paul could be accusing Gentile, pagan women of indulging in what would be seen by Jewish contemporaries as excessive, unnatural intercourse with men.

And this is also how some of the earliest Christian commentators, including Augustine and Ambrosiaster, understood the passage.

But what about the men? Surely this is clear. Paul is condemning men having sex with men.

Except the passage does not say men. It says, 'males with males'. This is not a pedantic, minor difference, but a significant one. Why? Because 'males' was a word often used deliberately in the Graeco-Roman world in connection with pederasty, as the term covered boys as well as men.

As I've already shown, pederasty was widely accepted by the Graeco-Roman world. This abuse of boys by men was by far the most common form of male same-sex activity. It was also closely associated with idolatry in Jewish thought at the time.

We can interpret the passage, therefore, far differently from condemning lesbian and homosexual people. Instead, it is condemning rampant, uncontrolled lust and abuse of boys. Interpreting the passage in this way makes sense in the context of the ancient world and also in the context of Paul's rhetorical aims.

But there is also a way of reading which not only takes this aspect seriously, but makes sense of the whole passage, and was the way that some of the earliest Christian commentators understood it.

Let us remind ourselves of Paul's argument. The critical failing of Gentiles (*not* all humanity) was idolatry; worshipping creation, not the creator.

Pagan worship at the time of Paul included a range of goddesses associated with fertility, like Artemis, Aphrodite, Isis, Ceres and Cybele.

You may be familiar with Artemis from Paul's difficulties in Ephesus. Residents worried Paul was diminishing the temple dedicated to her there and also affecting economic trade in silver shrines (see Acts 19:23–41). At the time, the temple to Artemis at Ephesus was one of the seven wonders of the ancient world; a massive construction over 60 feet tall and 450 feet long. The worship of Artemis, also called Diana, was embedded in the life of the ancient world.

You may be less familiar with the goddess Cybele, but she was important to Rome. Known as the 'Great Mother' (*magna mater*), she was seen as the divine protector of the city of Rome. Worship of Cybele had been supported in Rome by the wife of Augustus Caesar.

What did worship of fertility goddesses like Artemis and Cybele involve? The following ancient description is dependent upon people criticising pagan worship. As a result, it is hard to know how close to reality it is. Real life may have been much tamer and more boring than the description that follows.

However, the descriptions do reveal what people were writing and saying about pagan worship, and this is what Paul taps into in Romans.

The accounts are graphic.

The cult of Cybele (and other fertility cults were similar) was said to involve priestesses who, during ecstatic, orgiastic celebrations, would use phalluses to penetrate each other and also to penetrate male followers called *galli*. These *galli* would also penetrate each other whilst cross dressing. The *galli* would also, it was claimed, castrate themselves as part of ecstatic worship at festival time.

As an example, here is the account of Lucian (2nd C AD):

> During these days they are made Galli. As the Galli sing and celebrate their orgies, frenzy falls on many of them and many who had come as mere spectators afterwards are found to have committed the great act. I will narrate what they do. Any young man who has resolved on this action, strips off his clothes, and with a loud shout bursts into the midst of the crowd, and picks up a sword from a number of swords which I suppose have been kept ready for many years for this purpose. He takes it and castrates himself and then runs wild through the city, bearing in his hands what he has cut off. He casts it into any house at will, and from this house he receives women's raiment and ornaments. Thus they act during their ceremonies of castration.
>
> — LUCIAN, *SYR. D.* 51

How does this fit in with Romans? Look again at Romans 1:26–27. Remember that Paul is writing about idolatry (in keeping with his earlier references).

Someone from Paul's culture and time, hearing Romans,

would associate the language with the ecstatic worship of goddesses.

> On account of this [the Gentile idolatry] God handed them over to dishonourable passions: for both their females exchanged the natural usage for the usage against nature...
>
> — ROMANS 1:26

Seeing pagan fertility goddess worship as the context explains why Paul mentions females first: they were the priestesses in charge of the cult. The exchange to a 'usage against nature' is a reference to the priestesses using phalluses to penetrate both each other and the *galli*.

> ...likewise also the males, having left the natural usage of females, were burnt up in their desire for each other, males in males doing that which brought shame and receiving in themselves the due rewards which inevitably came from their going astray.
>
> — ROMANS 1:27

The context of goddess worship also explains Paul's reference to the males burning in desire for each other: the male *galli* penetrated each other as part of the orgiastic worship.

It further explains the 'due rewards' having already been received; this is a reference to self-castration as part of frenzied worship.

And, just as in other similar Jewish writings, this condemnation of frenzied pagan worship is followed up by general accusations of all sorts of wickedness.

Understanding the passage this way also fits Paul's rhetorical aims. Pagan worship is something clearly accepted in the

Gentile world, not only accepted, but integral to it, but not accepted by Jewish people. It is therefore perfect for springing the trap upon the Jewish hearer.

Furthermore, understanding the passage this way also sees it following a similar pattern to that found elsewhere in Jewish writings, which begin with the problems of idolatry and then widen the concerns to all sorts of evils (see Wisdom 14:23–29).

Let us recap the different possibilities for understanding Romans 1:26–28. Any interpretation should:

- make sense of Paul's Jewish background;
- criticise practices that are identified with pagans but not Jewish people;
- fit in with Paul's framing of the argument as idolatry;
- explain why Paul starts with women, not men;
- match the earliest Christian understandings of Romans.

When we consider this list, what may initially have seemed an 'obvious' reading that Paul was referring to gay and lesbian people falls apart. No-one, pagan or Jewish, categorised sexuality this way. If they had been able to, they were not associated exclusively with pagan culture; they do not really fit the framing as idolatry; there is no explanation of why Paul mentions women first; and this is not how the passage was first understood by Christians.

The idea that Paul was writing about female and male same-sex activity, not orientation, is stronger. It makes sense of Paul's Jewish background. Pederasty was associated with Gentile rather than Jewish practice, although this is not particularly true of female same-sex activity. It sort of fits Paul's argument from idolatry, if you see it as a distortion of the creation in Genesis. However, it does not explain why females are mentioned first by Paul. Additionally, this interpretation of

Romans cannot be found amongst Christian writings until the late fourth century.

What about the interpretation that Paul is referring to females having unnatural intercourse with males, and pederasty?

This fits Paul's Jewish background, and uses accusations that are specific to pagans. It also fits with Paul's argument about idolatry, making some sense of females being named first: Paul is starting with male-female unnatural intercourse before moving to male-male pederasty. This interpretation also fits in with references to Romans in early Christian writings from the second century onwards.

Could Paul have been talking about pagan goddess worship? It fits Paul's Jewish background, uses accusations that are closely linked to pagans (particularly in Rome), is continuing the theme of idolatry, makes sense of why females, the priestesses, are named first, and matches the earliest Christian writings on Romans.

So, what is the plain meaning of Romans 1? To a first century person, it might have appeared plain that Paul was referring to frenzied sexual activity connected with fertility goddess worship. The idea that Paul was focusing on people with a particular sexual orientation would have seemed strange.

What may have seemed to ancient hearers a plain meaning of Paul's letter can be obscured to us because their world is different from ours. But if Paul is condemning pederasty, or idolatrous, ecstatic, orgiastic, self-harming pagan goddess worship, that is quite different from loving, faithful, committed relationships.

CHAPTER 9
THE CONTEXT OF CORINTH

If we often see Romans 1 as containing the most important verses in the Bible for debates around sexuality, Paul's first letter to the Corinthians comes as a close second. Does it say that those who are gay or lesbian are outside of God's kingdom? Is this not clear about the biblical perspective on sexuality?

As you might guess, the answer to both questions is no.

In 1 Corinthians 6:9–11, Paul writes about a variety of wrong-doers who will not inherit God's kingdom. Included in the list are a couple of words that the New International Version (NIV) of the Bible translates as 'men who have sex with men' and the English Standard Version (ESV) translates as 'men who practice homosexuality'.

However, the King James version of the Bible (KJV) has 'effeminate' and 'abusers of themselves with mankind'.

What is going on here?

We need to have a closer look at the verses in question. Here is another version, the New Revised Standard Version (NRSV), with another translation, this time 'male prostitutes' and 'sodomites' are used:

Do you not know that wrongdoers will not inherit the kingdom of God? Do not be deceived! Fornicators, idolaters, adulterers, male prostitutes, sodomites, thieves, the greedy, drunkards, revilers, robbers—none of these will inherit the kingdom of God. And this is what some of you used to be. But you were washed, you were sanctified, you were justified in the name of the Lord Jesus Christ and in the Spirit of our God.

— 1 CORINTHIANS 6:9–11

Let us dig a little into some of the terms in that list. 'Fornicators' is a translation of the Greek word *pornoi*, a word which particularly suggests the use of prostitutes, which was widespread in Roman times. Its use was broadening to mean excessive lust; another recent commentator suggested 'lechery' as an indication of what it covered.

'Idolaters' is straightforward. It picks up those who worship pagan gods and goddesses.

'Adulterers' translates *moichoi*. It covers a narrower meaning than the English translation suggests. As explained in previous chapters, legally, only sleeping with someone who could their honour violated was 'adultery'. Enslaved people and prostitutes legally had no honour, so sex with them did not constitute adultery. Only intercourse with a freeborn woman who was not your wife was legally adultery.

Then we come to the two key words: *malakoi* and *arsenokoitai*. Why is there so much disagreement about how to translate them?

Malakoi comes from the word, *malakos*, which literally means 'soft'. For example, in Matthew 11:8 Jesus compares John the Baptist to those who dress in soft robes and live in palaces (perhaps a dig at King Herod). The word for 'soft robes', *malaka*, comes from the same root.

72

In English, 'soft' can cover a range of meanings. If you call a pillow soft, you are talking about its physical qualities. But if you call a person soft, you are saying something about their character; that they are weak.

The Greek of Paul's day functioned in the same way. So *malakos* could mean effeminate, in a patriarchal society where to be seen as feminine meant others saw you as weaker and more swayed by your passions.

However, thinking of *malakos* as simply meaning effeminate can mislead us. Our idea of effeminacy is different from how people thought about it then.

In Roman times, it could refer to those who acted in a dissolute, debauched way.

This might include the cowardly, the lazy or the idle rich sleeping around with any women available.

Think of playboys, or eighteenth-century dandies. If a man spent too much time caring about how he looked, and acting on his lust, that was being soft; *malakos*.

The word could also refer to those who took the 'effeminate' position in intercourse. So, if you were the passive partner, the one being penetrated, you would be seen as *malakos*. Because of this, *malakos* could also be a term used for a male prostitute.

As you can see, *malakos* was a broad term, linked to what were seen as unmanly vices. This is perhaps why one of the very first English versions of the Bible, The Coverdale, translated it as 'weaklinges'.

Which one of these possibilities did Paul mean? In the letter, there are no clues to help us to narrow it down. It is just one term in a list of vices. This is why translations differ so much from one another.

Does *malakos* refer to the idle rich, to those who are sleeping with loads of women, to male prostitutes, or to some other aspect of the word? How much weight do we put on the next item in the list being *arsenokoitai*, the other disputed term which we are about to come to?

Different commentators disagree with each other, which is why we have so many different translations of this term.

My personal view is that Paul was referring in a general way to the morally weak; those who chose to let their lust lead their actions.

What about the other term, *arsenokoitai*, the plural form of *arsenokoitēs*? We have the mirror image of the problem we had with *malakos*. There, the issue is of a word widely used in Greek literature, but with a variety of meanings. With this term, Paul's use of the word in 1 Corinthians is the earliest we have on record by any ancient writer. It was only infrequently used afterwards, and often only when people were quoting Paul directly. So, what did Paul mean by this word?

One approach is to look at what the different parts of the word might be able to tell us. *Arsenokoitēs* has two halves:

- *arseno* comes from a word meaning 'male' (not the same as a man);
- *koitēs* comes from a word meaning 'bed', but in Greek as in English 'bed' was sometimes a euphemism for sex (this is where we get our word 'coitus' from).

Putting the two together suggests a 'male-bedder'.

But we need to be cautious here. Working out meanings this way can be dangerous. Cupboards do not necessarily have cups inside. Butterflies do not contain butter.

We may have another clue in working out where Paul might have got the word from. One possibility is from the Greek version of Leviticus 20:13. Here, you get together in the same sentence the words *arsenos* (male) and *koitēn* (bed). This may tell us more about the history of the word, but it does not tell us how it was used in practice.

We are working with limited evidence.

If we just look at how the word is constructed, and its possible source from Leviticus, it looks like the word refers to those who bed males.

In the Graeco-Roman world of Paul's time, overwhelmingly the most common form of bedding males was the violation of boys: pederasty. The boys were usually enslaved, prostitutes or both.

Whenever the Jewish writer Philo, a rough contemporary of Paul, refers to male-male intercourse, he means with boys (when he does not refer to practices associated with goddess worship).

This means that if someone in Corinth heard 'male-bedder', they would assume that pederasty was meant.

We do have a little more evidence from how writers used the word in the immediate years after Paul. Here, some use *arsenokoitēs* in contexts which suggest that violent, economic oppression may also have been part of its meaning.

As an example, some of the earliest occurrences outside of the Bible include it in lists of economic vices rather than sexual ones.

Given the thriving slave trade in boy prostitutes in the ancient world, perhaps this is not surprising.

The word is also used in 1 Timothy:

This means understanding that the law is laid down not for the innocent but for the lawless and disobedient, for the godless and sinful, for the unholy and profane, for those who kill their father or mother, for murderers, fornicators (*pornois*), sodomites (*arsenokoitais*), slave traders (*andrapodistais*), liars, perjurers, and whatever else is contrary to the sound teaching that conforms to the glorious gospel of the blessed God, which he entrusted to me.

— 1 TIMOTHY 1:9–11

Here, the word is sandwiched between a word for sexual immorality, and a word for economic evil. One way of interpreting the list is that it is naming those who sleep around, particularly with prostitutes, those who use boys who were enslaved prostitutes, and those who buy and sell the enslaved prostitutes.

Other early Christian literature also suggests that Paul was referring to pederasty. Some of them contain similar lists of vices to those in Paul's letter, but use a word meaning child corruption (*paidophthoria*) to refer to pederasty directly. Here is a selection spanning the first four centuries of Christianity:

You shall not murder; you shall not commit adultery; you shall not corrupt children [*paidophthorēseis*]; you shall not be sexually immoral; you shall not steal...

— *DIDACHE* 2.2 (2ND CENTURY TEACHING MANUAL)

You shall not be sexually immoral; you shall not commit adultery; you shall not corrupt children [*paidophthorēseis*].

— *BARNABAS* 19.4 (2ND CENTURY LETTER)

...how much more shall all the nations appear to be under a curse who practise idolatry, who corrupt children [*paidophthorounta*], and commit other crimes?

— JUSTIN MARTYR, *DIAL. TRYPHO* 95 (2ND
CENTURY CHRISTIAN WRITING)

You shall not commit adultery. You shall not worship idols. You shall not corrupt children [*paidophthorēseis*]. You shall not steal...

— CLEMENT OF ALEXANDRIA, *PAEDAGOGUS*
3.12 (EARLY 3RD CENTURY)

Which is more beautiful? To confess the cross, or to attribute to those you call gods adultery and corruption of children [*paidophthorias*]?

— ATHANASIUS, *VITA ANTONII* 74 (EARLY 4TH
CENTURY)

One who approves of adulteries and corruption of children [*paidophthorias*]...

— GREGORY OF NAZIANZEN, *ADV.*
EUNOMIANOS (ORAT. 27) 6. (LATE 4TH
CENTURY)

Notice that these are general lists summing up a wide range of wicked activities in a broad way. Pederasty was so common that it appears as a main item in many lists. And, in some cases, the lists have a threefold attack on sexual immorality: do not sleep around, do not commit adultery, do not commit pederasty.

I think Paul's list in 1 Corinthians is the same. Do not sleep around, do not commit adultery, do not commit pederasty. The only difference is that, where these writers used 'child corruption' to refer to pederasty, Paul used 'male-bedders'.

In other words, 'male-bedders' means violating boys.

Can I prove this? No. We simply do not have enough evidence to prove beyond reasonable doubt *any* interpretation of the word *arsenokoitai*. But I do think it is probable that when Paul used this term the abuse of boys was uppermost in his mind and in the minds of those hearing the letter in Corinth.

Additionally, any translation that uses the word 'homosexual' is misleading. The word to us suggests an orientation, that the person will generally only find people of the same sex attractive.

As earlier chapters have shown, this is not the way that sexuality was constructed. In the Roman world, what was considered important was whether you were the active, dominant party or the passive, submissive party. Those committing pederasty were not putting their masculinity at risk. If anything the reverse was true. They would equally abuse prostitutes and female enslaved people, whilst remaining respected, married members of the community.

Looking again at 1 Corinthians, Paul appears to have been condemning those who were morally lax, and those who abused boys.

It hardly needs saying (but I shall anyway) that this is an utterly different focus from that of two people wishing to form a faithful, committed, lifelong relationship.

CHAPTER 10
JUDE THE OBSCURE

ON RARE OCCASIONS, people ask me about particular verses in Jude, which they have been told 'prove' that Sodom's sin was homosexuality.

Jude is a small book in the New Testament, and sometimes neglected in comparison to other parts. One might even call it obscure, to riff on Thomas Hardy. If the book is little known, so is some of its background.

Perhaps this is why I am only occasionally asked to consider these verses. In this chapter, I shall explain why the most probable reading is that Jude is not referring to any type of homosexuality or same-sex intercourse.

What does Jude say about Sodom? The key verses are these:

And the angels who did not keep their own position, but left their proper dwelling, he has kept in eternal chains in deepest darkness for the judgment of the great Day. Likewise, Sodom and Gomorrah and the surrounding cities, which, in the same manner as they, indulged in sexual immorality [*ekporneusasai*] and pursued unnatural lust [*sarkos heteras*], serve as an example by undergoing a punishment of eternal fire.

I have shown the Greek transliterated for a couple of words here, because they help us understand more precisely what is being said.

The first, translated above as 'indulged in sexual immorality', is *ekporneusasai*. We have come across variants of this word before. The stem of the word (*porn*) originally referred to prostitution, but its meaning was widening to encompass uncontrolled lust and lechery. This is a general term, which is not specifically linked to same-sex activity.

However, it is the second part of the verse which some focus on. Here, the words 'unnatural lust' are given as the translation for *sarkos heteras*. A more literal translation would be that they pursued 'other flesh'. What might this mean?

At once, we can notice that this is a strange construction to choose if Jude is referring to homosexuality of any sort. That would not be pursuing *other* flesh, but the *same* sort of flesh.

We also need to pay attention to the previous verse. Sodom and Gomorrah are not just picked out to highlight a sin, but because they sinned 'in the same manner' as angels who did not keep their own station. The mention of angels reminds us of a key feature of the account in Genesis of Sodom: the visitors to Lot were angels sent by God.

At this point, many of us will have a hard time working out to what Jude could be referring, because we have little familiarity with some of the Jewish writings of the time.

In particular, Jude shares many features with the book of 1 Enoch (an ancient Jewish apocalyptic text that is considered part of the Bible by some Ethiopian churches). Jude 14–15 even quotes 1 Enoch 1:9.

1 Enoch includes an account of two hundred angels falling

from heaven. These angels then take human wives, in what builds on Genesis 6:1–2:

> And it came to pass, when the sons of men had increased, that in those days there were born to them fair and beautiful daughters. And the angels, the sons of heaven, saw them and desired them.
>
> And they said to one another: 'Come, let us choose for ourselves wives from the children of men, and let us beget for ourselves children.'
>
> And Semyaza, who was their leader, said to them: 'I fear that you may not wish this deed to be done, and that I alone will pay for this great sin.' And they all answered him and said: 'Let us all swear an oath, and bind one another with curses not to alter this plan, but to carry out this plan effectively.' Then they all swore together, and all bound one another with curses to it.
>
> And they were in all two hundred, and they came down on Ardis which is the summit of Mount Hermon. And they called the mountain Hermon, because on it they swore and bound one another with curses. And these are the names of their leaders: Semyaza, who was their leader, Urakiba, Ramiel, Kokabiel, Tamiel, Ramiel, Daniel, Ezeqiel, Baraqiel, Asael, Armaros, Batriel, Ananel, Zaqiel, Samsiel, Sartael, Turiel, Yomiel, Araziel. These are the leaders of the two hundred angels, and of all the others with them.
>
> —1 ENOCH 6 (TRANS. BY KNIBB, 1978)

Jude therefore appears to be referring to the sin of angels and humans (who are 'other flesh' from each other) having, or attempting to have, intercourse together.

To put it more simply, Jude condemns the people of Sodom and Gomorrah for attempting to have intercourse with angels, just as angels were condemned in 1 Enoch for seeking intercourse with humans. It has nothing to do with homosexuality.

With this examination of Jude, we have completed our tour around the Bible of the passages normally used to condemn homosexuality.

In each case, a closer examination shows that the Bible is not addressing the situation we are considering now: mutual, faithful loving relationships between people of the same sex.

However, sexuality is not the only issue that is 'live' in this debate: you may also have been told that the Bible means that people should not transition from one gender to another; that being transgender is sinful. The next chapter addresses this issue.

CHAPTER 11

WHAT DOES THE BIBLE SAY ABOUT TRANSGENDER PEOPLE?

THIS TOPIC IS the one that always surprises me. Not because of issues to do with gender, but because of the poor quality of argument generally put up against being transgender.

I have frequently found that non-affirming contributors base their argument on three building blocks, often claiming these are Biblical principles. Their arguments actually sit lightly to the Bible, so you may be disappointed to find limited engagement with specific scriptures.

In this chapter, I am going to explain why I consider the arguments so poor. Along the way, we will also look at issues to do with people who are intersex. In other words, we will cover the 'TI' of LGBTQI+.

Before we dive in, I need to stress that people who are transgender are not the same as people who are intersex, and vice versa. The two need to be treated separately. However, both are brought into this chapter because of shared issues concerning gender.

We also need to do some preliminary work on the terms that are being used. Some of you may be familiar with all of this, but to others this may be first time that you come across some of these terms. They are useful in that they enable us to separate out different aspects which are important.

We begin with *gender identity*. This is how you think of yourself. In my mind, I think of myself as a man. That is my gender identity. Most people's gender identity gets fixed at a young age. Some sociologists call it a primary identity.

Gender expression is how your gender comes over in how you live, behave, what you wear and how you speak. For example, I do not wear skirts, because in my culture that sends out female gender signals.

Gender expression varies from country to country and culture to culture. For example, some years ago my baby daughters were mistaken for boys in Spain when we were there on holiday. Why? They were dressed in pink, and in England everyone would assume they were girls. However, they did not have their ears pierced, and in Spain, most baby girls have their ears pierced. Therefore, the people we met thought our girls must be boys. That is one example of how gender expression varies from place to place.

Gender expression can be conscious, but it is often unconscious or subconscious. We may not think about how we walk or talk, or why we wear certain clothes, but all will still exhibit to some degree our gender expression.

Biological sex refers to the physical characteristics of being male or female. This includes genitalia and body shape, but also includes chromosomes, and hormones, and even your physical brain structure.

Someone who is *transgender* is a person whose gender identity and biological sex don't align. Often (but not always) they may *transition* from the gender associated with their biological sex to the other. Therefore, a trans woman is someone who used to be identified as a male, but identifies, and expresses their gender, as a female.

If you did chemistry, you may remember that some molecules can exist in two different forms that are mirror images of each other. In science, these are called the cis- and trans- forms of the molecule.

Similar language has been adopted where it is helpful to distinguish between those who are transgender and those who are not. So, a *cisgender* man is a man who has always identified as a male, and feels their gender identity aligns with their biological sex, whereas a transgender man is someone who was assigned female at birth but identifies as a man. Sometimes the terms 'cis' and 'trans' are used as a shorthand.

There are more terms that are in use, such as non-binary, genderqueer, gender fluid and many more. However, for the rest of this chapter we'll stick to looking at transgender people and the Bible.

That is the terminology. Now we can start looking at the objections. The three building blocks used in most arguments are these:

- God made us male and female, two distinct genders.
- God does not make mistakes, so your gender identity needs to match your biological sex.
- Gender confusion is bad, because God made males and females distinct, and those differences should not be blurred.

What is the response if someone has a gender identity that is different from their assigned sex at birth? The response is usually along the lines of: well, that is regrettable, and we must be compassionate, but gender dysphoria is a mental health problem and should be addressed by encouraging the person to identify with their assigned sex.

Let us examine each of the three building blocks in turn.

We begin with the assertion that God made two distinct genders; male and female.

The passages in the Bible which are usually referred to at this point are the creation accounts of Genesis 1–2. Those proposing this may also bring in other passages which refer back to Genesis, for example, the comments of Jesus about marriage in Matthew 19:3–12 and Mark 10:2–12.

On closer examination, this is a strange use of Genesis 1–2. To say that God only made a male and a female, and that this must apply to everyone since, is going beyond what the text says.

Of course, it does apply to the vast majority of people. According to studies, only about 1 in 5,000 to 1 in 10,000 of the population identify as transgender. The creation accounts in Genesis are not focused on unusual situations. For example, they do not even apply in a straightforward way to those people who do not have children, or who remain single.

The creation accounts confirm that God blesses both male and female, and that both are made in his image. They also confirm that God blesses marriage and children. But Genesis does not try to address being transgender, whether you must get married, or whether you must have children. Genesis does not address being transgender directly at all.

There are further difficulties. The claim is that there are two, and only two, completely distinct biological sexes. Again, this is true for most people, but it is not true for everyone. Here, we need to consider people who are intersex.

Just to reiterate, people who are intersex are not people who are transgender. In that case, what does being intersex mean?

Put simply, there are a number of markers of biological sex. For example, chromosomes, which carry your DNA, are a marker. One set of pairs (humans usually have 23 pairs) are called the sex chromosomes, and usually the chromosome is designated as either X or Y. People who have a pair of XX chromosomes are usually female. People who have an XY pairing are usually male.

But our biology is not just affected by our DNA. Hormones have a massive influence over how our bodies develop in the womb, and then later at puberty.

We also need to consider what our bodies actually look like: what shape we are; what genitalia we have.

There is also some research to show that physical brain structure also varies between females and males.

All of these are separate from our sense of identity, but all go into what biological sex we are assigned at birth.

Usually, all of these line up neatly.

For example, someone with XY chromosomes then gets hormones for male development in the womb, and subsequently is born with male genitalia. At puberty hormones mean that the body grows into a typical male shape. And most males will also have a sense of identity that matches. The same is mostly true for females with XX chromosomes.

But it does not always work out this way. Occasionally, you get women who are born with XY chromosomes. From birth, they have the external physical body of a female, and usually identify as female. They may go through their lives completely unaware of this, never knowing that their chromosomes are not typically female. How come?

This can happen when bodies do not react in the womb to a hormone called androgen (the condition is called androgen insensitivity syndrome, or AIS). These women with XY chromosomes are just one example of being intersex.

You can also get a similar condition in men. These are people who have male bodies from birth and identify as males, but whose chromosomes are XX (this is called XX male syndrome).

There is even the situation where people may have XY chromosomes that are typically male, but they are born appearing female. Their body then changes at puberty into a male one (this is called 5α-reductase deficiency).

Beyond these examples, there are a wide range of conditions where the body may have some typically male biological characteristics, and some typically female biological characteristics. There are also a range of conditions where people do not have 46 chromosomes, and may have, for example, XXY chromosomes.

Broadly, people with these features, where not all the biological markers line up together neatly, come under the intersex category (the I in LGBTQI+).

The conditions are rare, but their existence shows clearly that there is no single biological marker that you can point to in order to identify someone as male or female definitively. Chromosomes, hormones, brain structure and physical appearance do not always line up together neatly. It is scientifically wrong to say that the biological sexes are always distinct.

Intersex people are not addressed directly in scripture at all. So, how do some non-affirming commentators handle the reality of intersex people?

I am afraid that often intersex people are ignored entirely. Others argue that their existence is a result of the fall, that it is a groaning of creation (referencing Romans 8), and that in any case, they are exceptions.

However, both of these inadequate responses are put into the shade by the cruel response of some commentators.

Some non-affirming evangelicals insist that people with conditions like androgen insensitivity syndrome should live out their lives according to their genotype (that is, according to their chromosomes), with support and medical intervention to help them.

In other words, for example, grown women who find out that they have a genetic condition like AIS are being told they now should live the rest of their lives as men, and should only marry women.

Let me be blunt. This is toxic advice. It is advocating conversion therapy including surgery simply because some people fail to fit a particular, recent definition of biological sex.

Before the discovery of DNA, people with this condition would go through their entire lives with no-one questioning their biological sex. We have no idea of the genetic makeup of any of the people through history up to the twentieth century. By this strange logic, we do not know whether we should call Jesus or Paul male, or Mary Magdalene female, because we do not have access to their chromosomes.

People with androgen insensitivity syndrome have been female from birth, brought up as female, with female bodies, and identify as female, and are being told to have surgery to make themselves into men. The suggestion is shameful, unless it is something the person wants to do of their own free will to assert their gender identity.

If people who are intersex do not fit neatly into strict categories, neither do those who are transgender or who are seeking to transition. Some people have a deep-seated, permanent sense that their gender identity is different from the one assigned at birth. This is called 'gender dysphoria'.

We do not know why exactly this happens, but it is at least partly biological in cause. Gender identity, therefore, is also part of biological sex.

We know that it is at least partly biological, and in fact genetic, from twin studies. If an identical twin (the technical term is monozygotic) transitions, there is a 20–30% chance that their sibling, with the same DNA, will also transition. If a non-identical (dizygotic) twin transitions, the chance that their sibling, sharing 50% of the same DNA and the same womb and upbringing, drops to 2% or lower.

An additional piece of evidence that gender identity is

biological comes from the study of physical brain structure. Here, some studies have suggested that a person's physical brain structure is more likely to resemble their preferred gender identity rather than the sex assigned at birth. This evidence is less conclusive, though.

The similarity between intersex and transgender people comes from a misalignment of all the multiple indicators of gender.

The scientific evidence is clear. The first building block is simply wrong. While most people do fit into two distinct genders, there are some people, such as trans people, who do not fit neatly into one distinct gender, or feel as if their gender identity misaligns with their assigned sex.

The second building block is the belief that God does not make mistakes, and therefore your gender identity ought to match your biological sex.

This makes no sense to me on a number of different levels. For example, it is difficult to see how this applies to intersex people. If God creates them as part of a good creation (which I actually do believe), and they are part of the variety that God looks upon and declares good, then why cannot trans people be in the same position?

But if, as some claim, intersex people are the result of the fall, and therefore an exception for whom allowances must be made, then again, why cannot we do the same with trans people?

The slogan 'God does not make mistakes' therefore becomes devoid of any real meaning. It is just an empty slogan.

There is a further issue, in any case, with this slogan. If there is a mismatch between gender identity and the physical body, why should the physical body take priority over the mind and sense of identity?

I have sometimes seen this expressed by non-affirming commentators as comparing feelings with being, or psychology compared with ontology. But this is not taking our sense of self seriously enough, and taking our bodies too seriously.

Yes, we need to take our physical bodies seriously; we follow a Christ who took human flesh, who became incarnate. Our bodies are real. But so is what is going on inside us. Our minds are real too.

It only takes a moment to realise that this must be so. Our identity in Christ is not just 'feelings' or 'psychology' but our ultimate reality. Trying to reduce biology to being the only reality is sub-Christian, a type of materialism.

This approach even fails on its own terms. We have already seen that being trans is at least partly based on biology, that there are genetic causes lying behind it to some extent. Therefore, you cannot separate being trans from the biological body.

If, then, there is a mismatch between the body and the identity, why privilege the body over the sense of identity? This is not something that scripture tells us to do. It is something being imposed externally on scripture, that is being read into the Bible.

If someone has a strong, abiding, permanent sense of one gender identity, there is nothing in scripture to say that they should not seek to bring their body to align with their gender identity rather than the reverse.

The second building block, that biological sex ought to take priority, is not biblical. It is just an assumption, and a poor one at that.

The third building block of the argument is that gender confusion is always wrong. This in itself is an assumption, and issues to do with cultural expressions of gender identity tend to be ignored. Sometimes, those who are non-affirming point to Genesis 1, and the way that God separates night from day, sea from land, and made male and female. This sounds superficially convincing, but ignores reality. Night and day are different, but not distinct. Dawn and dusk are in-between times, as the day gradually lightens or darkens. There is no clear distinction between night and day. The same is true of sea and land, as anyone who has been on a beach holiday can tell.

However, I shall not dwell on this point, because *on its own terms* the argument against transitioning fails.

People who are trans have not chosen to have a mismatch between their gender identity and their biological sex. They haven't gone seeking any 'confusion' if you want to use that loaded term.

Instead, they are people who are trying to bring their reality more into alignment. They are bringing their gender expression and possibly also their biological sex into line with their gender identity. If they can be accused of anything, it is of seeking to reduce 'confusion'.

Let us return to those three building blocks.

God made male and female, but he also made people who are intersex and people who are transgender. Scripture does not address these situations directly.

Should our biological sex take priority over our sense of identity? Gender identity turns out to be at least partly biological, but in any case, scripture does not tell us that our bodies must take priority. That is something imposed on scripture.

Is gender confusion wrong? This is a loaded way of asking the question, but even so, transitioning is a way of bringing gender identity, gender expression and biological sex more into line with one another. That is not causing confusion, but rather addressing confusion.

The three building blocks turn out to be based on a foundation of sand, washed away by clear thinking and scripture.

What, therefore, does the Bible say about transgender people? Directly, not a lot, despite how voluble some non-affirming commentators may be.

There are some verses that are pointed to beyond Genesis,

which are worth addressing briefly. One of these is from Deuteronomy:

> A woman shall not wear a man's apparel, nor shall a man put on a woman's garment; for whoever does such things is abhorrent to the LORD your God.

> — DEUTERONOMY 22:5

It is first worth noting that this verse could only be relevant to people who are transgender if you assume that a trans man is 'really' a woman or vice versa. However, this is precisely what is at stake: how do we decide whether someone is a man or a woman, when biology and identity do not match? The verse is an example of the type often used to condemn 'gender confusion', but it is not an appropriate criticism of those who are transgender.

Secondly, it is far from clear what the context of this verse is. For example, many of the cultures surrounding Israel had religious practices that included pagan priests who cross-dressed. Cross-dressing, therefore, became a symbol of idolatry.

Whatever the original context, it is highly unlikely that either the writer, or the original audience, would have had people who are transgender in mind.

A broader biblical area where there are some parallels concerns eunuchs. The New Testament generally appears positive towards those who were eunuchs (for example, Acts 8:26–40). Although these passages are a rich resource for those who are transgender, I have not considered them closely in this book, because the two categories (transgender and eunuch) are separate, even if related in some areas. People who were eunuchs were not transgender, and vice versa.

To return to our main concern, the Bible cannot therefore be said to condemn people who are transgender, or to suggest that being transgender or transitioning is wrong. Arguments that the Bible does do that are based on spurious appeals to Genesis and often ignore both science and logic.

But if the Bible does not condemn people who are transgender, or loving, faithful same-sex relationships, is there anything positive in the Bible to affirm such a position? The next chapter explores this area.

CHAPTER 12
AN INCLUSIVE BIBLE

THE STORY of the Bible is exclusive. God chooses one nation out of many, Israel, with whom God makes a covenant (Genesis 12).

The story of the Bible is inclusive. God chooses one nation out of many, Israel, through whom all the nations of the world will be blessed (Genesis 12).

Both strands can be found intertwined throughout the story of the people of God, culminating in the coming of Jesus. Jesus is the seed of Abraham so that through him all the blessings promised to the offspring of Abraham can be received (Galatians 3:6–16).

You and I are beneficiaries of that inclusive blessing. In particular, we are beneficiaries of the early church coming to realise that God's blessing was falling, not just upon Jewish people, but upon Gentiles.

A few of us might be Jewish Christians, sometimes known as messianic Jews, but most of us are people with no Jewish heritage.

The Bible tells us how that opening up happened, how the early church came to accept Gentiles. The account starts in Acts 10.

We are first introduced to Cornelius, an upright Roman

centurion living in Caesarea. An angel visits him in a vision, telling him to send for Simon Peter, hereafter referred to as Peter. Cornelius sends off a party of three to fetch Peter, who is in a different city called Joppa.

Meanwhile, Peter has a vision as he is waiting for lunch.

Before we look at what happens to Peter, I want you to conjure up in your mind your least favourite food. For me, it is baked beans. Even the look of them is unappealing to me. The smell makes me turn away, and I could not imagine forcing a single bean down my throat. As you have gathered, I cannot stand them.

I don't know what you chose. I have a friend who cannot abide custard.

The revulsion that we might feel on being faced with our least favourite food is still probably nothing to what Peter is about to encounter.

He sees a giant sheet being lowered down with various kinds of animals, and is told to kill and eat. Peter refuses, because the animals are not kosher—he would never dream of eating anything unclean. In the vision, he is admonished: 'What God has made clean, you must not call profane' (Acts 10:15). Peter experiences this three times.

It is easy to skip past this, and not sit with how astonishing this must have been for Peter.

His refusal to eat goes far beyond mere dislike. Everything in his whole life, every mealtime experience, has instilled in him that you do not eat certain foods—ever. Unclean foods are taboo. Jewish families told each other stories from the Maccabean wars of martyrs who chose death rather than eat pork.

To eat food that was not kosher would be to betray his people, his history, and God.

The command only to eat kosher food, that certain animals

were unclean, comes from the Torah. The plain meaning of scripture was clear: you do not eat some foods.

As Peter is puzzling over the dream, the party from Cornelius arrive. Peter and a few others return with them to Caesarea, and to Cornelius who has packed out his house with family and friends.

Here we get the first breakthrough that will ultimately lead to Gentiles belonging to the church.

You would think that what Peter would learn from his vision is that all food is clean. It would no longer matter whether, for example, a plate of meat included pork.

This by itself would be a seismic split from the past, a repudiation of part of what it had always meant to be faithful to God.

That is not the lesson that Peter learns.

Peter makes a theological leap of the imagination, and declares:

> God has shown me that I should not call anyone profane or unclean.

> — ACTS 10:28

It is *people* who are no longer to be considered unclean, not just types of food.

The account in Acts then relates how, while Peter testifies about Jesus, the Holy Spirit falls on those listening. Peter's Jewish companions are amazed. Peter orders that the Gentile believers should be baptised.

Peter's decision was not accepted at once by others, who criticised him for taking this step. Peter's response was to argue that if the Holy Spirit had been given to the Gentiles, who was he to hinder God (Acts 11:17)?

We are therefore given a template in Acts. God has declared

all people clean. If God chooses to work in people, then we are not to hinder God.

You will already know where I am going with this. If God is at work in people who identify as LGBTQI+, then who are we to hinder God?

However, some of you may have formed objections to using Acts in this way. Let me try to address these.

One objection might be that the acceptance took place after the first Christian leaders gathered together, confirmed that it was in keeping with scripture, and set out some basic rules for the Gentiles to follow, one of which was to avoid sexual immorality.

Same-sex intercourse, the argument goes, would be considered as sexual immorality. Therefore, it is wrong to use the account in Acts as a template for affirmation of people who are in same-sex relationships.

This is a serious objection, and deserves some space to consider it properly.

To understand what happened, we need to keep following the account in Acts. Some Christians followed Peter's lead; in particular, we are told about Barnabas and Saul, better known to us as Paul. From Paul's letters we know that he had been given a specific ministry as the apostle to the Gentiles.

However, some of the first Christians (who initially, we need to remind ourselves, were all Jewish) objected. We can see traces of this dispute in the chapters of Acts that follow the narrative of Cornelius and Peter, and in some of Paul's letters; particularly Galatians, Romans and Philippians.

Why did they object? It is highly likely that they believed Peter, and subsequently Paul and Barnabas, were ignoring scripture. To become part of the people of God was to enter into God's covenant with his people. Faithfulness to God was to be shown by faithfulness to the Torah, including circumcision for males and following food laws.

At some point, matters came to a head. Luke, with characteristic understatement, recounts that:

> Then certain individuals came down from Judea and were teaching the brothers, "Unless you are circumcised according to the custom of Moses, you cannot be saved." And after Paul and Barnabas had no small dissension and debate with them, Paul and Barnabas and some of the others were appointed to go up to Jerusalem to discuss this question with the apostles and the elders.
>
> — ACTS 15:1–2

This leads to the council of Jerusalem, where Peter, Barnabas and Paul end a debate on the matter by appealing to their experiences of God at work in the Gentiles. James decides that the Gentiles should not be forced to be circumcised and keep the law of Moses:

> My brothers, listen to me. Simeon has related how God first looked favourably on the Gentiles, to take from among them a people for his name. This agrees with the words of the prophets, as it is written, 'After this I will return, and I will rebuild the dwelling of David, which has fallen; from its ruins I will rebuild it, and I will set it up, so that all other peoples may seek the Lord—even all the Gentiles over whom my name has been called. Thus says the Lord, who has been making these things known from long ago.' Therefore I have reached the decision that we should not trouble those Gentiles who are turning to God, but we should write to them to abstain only from things polluted by idols and from fornication [*porneias*] and from whatever has been strangled and from blood.

A few points are worth highlighting here. First, experience is given a high priority. It is the testimony of Peter, Paul and Barnabas seeing God at work in the Gentiles which is important.

Secondly, James does use scripture in his justification of extending a welcome to the Gentiles. However, we would not be surprised if some of those involved did not find his interpretation here convincing. Perhaps they would accuse James of ignoring the plain sense of scripture, which made clear the expectation to follow the law of Moses. James is working with a trajectory within scripture, referring to a text which, with others, looked forward to the conversion of the nations. He does not feel constrained by existing understandings of what this might mean for the people of God.

Thirdly, there is a process of corporate prayerful discernment.

However, the main point, the one to which non-affirming Christians might direct our attention, rests in the particular instructions given to the Gentiles. These can also be found in Acts 15:29 and Acts 21:25.

The council instructs the Gentiles to abstain from four things. There are also some variant readings in different early manuscripts of Acts, but the ones following are generally considered most likely to be original:

- things polluted by idols;
- sexual immorality (translated as 'fornication' in the NRSV);
- strangled animals; and
- blood.

The argument from some non-affirming commentators is that these prohibitions include homosexuality, and therefore it is not appropriate to use the inclusion of the Gentiles as a basis for inclusion of people who are LGBTQI+.

This argument is based on three separate foundations, all of which are essential for the argument to work.

- The first foundation is that the prohibition is based on Leviticus 17 and 18, which includes the verse 18:22 addressed in chapter 5.
- The second foundation is that Leviticus 18:22 includes all forms of homosexuality within its scope.
- The third foundation is that the prohibitions in Acts cannot be changed.

Each foundation is less than solid.

Some scholars argue that the four prohibitions are a reference to Leviticus 17–18. These commands to the people of Israel are meant to apply not just to the Israelites, but also to the 'alien who resides' amongst them (Leviticus 18:26). Therefore there would be a logic in applying these laws to Gentiles who were being grafted into the people of God.

As Leviticus 18:22 is part of this section, some, therefore, argue that homosexuality is one of the prohibitions given to the Gentiles. These are the first two foundations in the argument.

However, this interpretation has serious problems. First, as the earlier chapter showed, you cannot simply apply what Leviticus was addressing to gay and lesbian relationships that we are discussing today. As already indicated, Jewish contemporaries of Paul such as Philo applied it to pederasty, a commonplace sexual activity in that context. And, of course, the verse says nothing at all about women and sexuality.

But secondly, it is a hotly contested point whether the prohibitions refer specifically to Leviticus, and this is a general divide amongst scholars, not one related to their positions on inclusion. For example, the first, most prominent prohibition is 'things polluted by idols'. The Greek term used here, *eidōlothuton*, does not occur in Leviticus 17–18. And whilst the prohibition on eating blood is in this section of Leviticus, there is nothing about animals that have been strangled.

A further cause for doubt is that the term used in the prohibitions for sexual immorality (*porneias*) is not used in Leviticus 17–18, and neither was it used generally in discussions about the prohibitions in Leviticus. These generally focused on incest, whereas in normal usage *porneia* originally was associated with prostitution, and was developing a broader meaning of sleeping around or lechery.

In other words, of the four prohibitions, only one clearly occurs in Leviticus 17–18. The others fit awkwardly at best.

An alternative explanation is that James was referring to the commands given to Noah (and hence for all humankind) after the flood. However, Genesis 9:3–4, again, does not refer to things polluted by idols, or to *porneia*.

If we want to know to what the decree was referring, we need to consider the context. The main Jewish critique of Gentiles was that they were pagan worshippers, bowing down to idols rather than the living God. The prohibitions could therefore target idolatry in general, and perhaps temple feasts in particular.

Let us take each prohibition in turn.

- *Things polluted by idols*: here, the reference may be to meat offered on altars and eaten within temple grounds. We see a similar concern in 1 Corinthians 8–10. Pagan temples operated to some extent as restaurants in the Roman world. Christians were to flee such settings.

- *Sexual immorality* (*porneia*): the roots of the term come from prostitution, including temple prostitution. In Jewish rhetoric, sexual immorality and temple worship were closely linked.
- *Strangled animals*: In some pagan temples, animals were choked as part of their sacrifice, offering up the life breath of the animal to the god or goddess.
- *Blood*: This could be a reference to priests drinking the blood of sacrificed animals, or more generally to the blood shed at such temples to pagan gods, which would also be considered polluting.

To summarise: there is a strong argument that the prohibitions were aimed at ensuring that the Gentiles did not return to pagan worship of idols. I should emphasise that this is not my own individual argument (though I think it the most probable); this is a mainstream understanding of Acts 15.

The first two foundations of the non-affirming argument are therefore extremely shaky. It is doubtful whether Leviticus is being specifically referred to here, and in any case, Leviticus is not addressing the issue we are facing today.

However, it is the third foundation which is weakest of all. For the sake of argument, let us suppose that the prohibitions do refer to Leviticus, and that the reference to blood and strangled animals are to do with food laws.

If that is the case, then it is abundantly clear that most of the Church has changed or ignored these prohibitions.

First of all, there is now no prohibition on eating meat containing blood.

At one time, I lived in Bury, Lancashire. The town is proud both of its market (proclaimed as world-famous), and also as a home for black pudding, a type of sausage where the key ingredient is blood (Germany has a similar type of sausage, called a *blutwurst*). Eating such a sausage would contravene not only the instructions in Leviticus 17-18, but also the direct, specific command mentioned in the Apostolic decree.

And I love black pudding. I consider a cooked breakfast underwhelming if it is lacking black pudding. I am not alone in this.

The Church does not condemn me for this. We do not get sermons preached on the evils of black pudding. Yet it ignores the prohibitions given to the Gentiles.

If we consider sexual immorality, then we also need to consider that according to Leviticus 17–18, intercourse while a woman is menstruating is sinful. If *porneia* covers Leviticus 18:22, it also includes Leviticus 18:19. Yet the Church does not condemn people for this, or preach on it, or consider it wrong at all.

Clearly, the Church is free to make further amendments and interpretations as to what is prohibited and what is permitted for Gentile believers.

The third foundation crumbles to dust.

At this point, it might be helpful to clarify exactly what I am claiming for the Acts 10–15 analogy, and what I am not.

I am claiming that the Acts 10–15 account shows that God's inclusion was far broader than the first disciples expected. I am claiming that the basis for extending inclusion to the Gentiles was the realisation that people and food considered impure were not considered so by God. I am claiming that seeing God at work in the Gentile believers was key in this change. And I am claiming that this change was seen to be in line with a trajectory of scripture, even though it seemed to contradict specific commands in the Torah.

On its own, this does not prove that the Church should accept same-sex marriage. But it does provide an authoritative analogy by which to judge the issue.

If we see God at work in gay and lesbian couples, if marriage helps them to flourish and love each other and others, if enabling mutual lifelong companionship is the most loving thing to do, if enabling someone to live as their gender identity is enabling them to live life to the fullest, then Acts gives the Church scriptural warrant for the full inclusion of people who are LGBTQI+.

Inclusion, if it follows God's work, is biblical. It is simply what the early Church did.

CHAPTER 13
LEARNING FROM HISTORY

Labels get tossed around frequently in the debates over sexuality and gender. Often, I have been accused of being, or labelled if you will, a revisionist. The implication is that I want to revise what the Church has traditionally taught.

I dislike this framing. One reason for my antipathy to the term is that it supposes that the Church has previously considered the issue in depth, and come to a considered, unified mind on the matter.

When it comes to issues around sexual orientation or gender identity, this simply is not the case. As outlined in Chapter two, the concepts of homosexuality or orientation were not used in the way the Graeco-Roman world of the New Testament thought or wrote about sexuality, instead focusing on issues of power and dominance in relationships.

It is therefore inappropriate to use the term 'revisionist', when there have been no clear arguments or thinking to revise. Effectively, our current debates are the first time the Church has seriously studied this issue.

However, there is a second reason I avoid using the term. It is because we are all revisionists.

That is a bold claim. How am I going to back it up?

By considering earlier Church debates on other issues.

We have already looked at one of these, the sinfulness or otherwise of lending money, in Chapter three. Most Christians in the West do not consider mortgages evil, or a car loan wrong, although they might well question the ethics of payday lenders. This is a revision, if you want to use that term, of Church teaching up until the Reformation, which was that all forms of moneylending were bad. So, when it comes to moneylending, we are revisionists.

However, we are also revisionists when it comes to slavery. Or at least, if we had been alive in the seventeenth and eighteenth century, we would have been accused of the equivalent terms then.

This may come as a surprise. Many Christians simply assume that it is clear that slavery is wrong ,and unbiblical, and that Christianity had a large part to play in making it illegal.

Both of those statements are true (in my opinion). But it is also an inconvenient, (shameful) truth, that many Christians fought for the legality of slavery, and justified it on biblical grounds.

Here, we are mainly talking about slavery in the Americas, although we will also touch on slavery in Britain.

Christian abolitionists in 1840s America struggled with finding a biblical mandate to end slavery. Jesus was silent on the issue, and Paul seemed, on the interpretations of the time, to favour those who owned enslaved people.

A 'plain-sense' reading of scripture seemed to favour the pro-slavery side. They could point to commands in the Old Testament which regulated slavery but did not prohibit it (Exodus 21:1–11; Leviticus 25:39–46 and Deuteronomy 15:12–18).

Within the New Testament, enslaved people were told to obey their owners as they obey Christ (Ephesians 6:5–9), to regard their owners as worthy of all honour (1 Timothy 6:1–2), that they should be submissive, faithful and not talk back (Titus 2:9–10), and that they should accept the authority of owners however kind or harsh (1 Peter 2:18–25). Finally, in Philemon, Paul sends a runaway fugitive back to their owner.

It was passages like these that convinced many that slavery as an institution was morally acceptable in principle. Supporters of slavery include a roll call of prominent Reformed evangelicals, amongst them James Thornwell, Robert Dabney and Charles Hodge. And they were equally convinced that abolitionists were ignoring the plain sense of scripture. As an example, here is Thornwell on abolitionists:

> The parties in the conflict are not merely abolitionists and slaveholders. They are atheists, socialists, communists, red republicans, Jacobins on the one side, and friends of order and regulated freedom on the other. In one word, the world is the battleground—Christianity and Atheism the combatants; and the progress of humanity at stake.
>
> — THORNWELL (1850, 14)

Thornwell was on the side of the Confederacy during this period, so perhaps it might be thought that this biased his viewpoint. However, Hodge was principal of Princeton Theological Seminary (1851–78), and wanted the abolition of slavery and the maintenance of the Union. Despite this, he too firmly believed that the Bible did not prohibit slavery in principle, and that such an approach undermined scripture:

> As it appears to us too clear to admit of either denial or doubt, that the scriptures do sanction slaveholding; that under the old dispensation it was expressly permitted by divine

command, and under the New Testament is no where forbidden or denounced, but on the contrary acknowledged to be consistent with the Christian character and profession (that is, consistent with justice, mercy, holiness, love to God and love to man), to declare it to be a heinous crime, is a direct impeachment of the word of God.

— HODGE (1836, 297–8)

This is not the place for a full exposition of the debates over slavery, but the broad outline is one where many prominent white evangelical scholars argued that slavery was biblical, and could point to a number of specific texts in support.

In contrast, those opposed relied on the general trajectory of the Bible, or the spirit of scripture. Again, here is Thornwell:

While they admit that the letter of the Scriptures is distinctly and unambiguously in our favour, they maintain that their spirit is against us.

— THORNWELL (1850, 16)

The result of this interpretation of scripture was that there was no real challenge to the biblical basis of slavery from white protestant seminaries during this critical period. What challenge there was came from people like Frederick Douglass, and before him Olaudah Equiano in Britain. What set them apart was a personal experience of enslavement, which led them to a different relationship with scripture and its relevance to slavery.

Abolitionists like Douglass had no specific anti-slavery texts to which they could turn. Instead, they argued from passages such as Galatians 3:28 ('There is no longer Jew or Greek, there is no longer slave or free, there is no longer male and female; for all of you are one in Christ Jesus') that the Bible preached a radical equality.

Douglass in particular used the Golden Rule (Matthew 7:12) as the key to how you should interpret the whole Bible. He explained his approach in a speech in England, where he also addressed accusations that he was either too extreme or anti-biblical. He responded:

> I have found it difficult to speak on this matter without persons coming forward and saying, "Douglass, are you not afraid of injuring the cause of Christ? You do not desire to do so, we know; but are you not undermining religion?" This has been said to me again and again, even since I came to this country, but I cannot be induced to leave off these exposures. I love the religion of our blessed Savior, I love that religion that comes from above, in the "wisdom of God, which is first pure, then peaceable, gentle, and easy to be entreated, full of mercy and good fruits, without partiality and without hypocrisy." I love that religion that sends its votaries to bind up the wounds of him that has fallen among thieves. I love that religion that makes it the duty of its disciples to visit the fatherless and widow in their affliction. I love that religion that is based upon the glorious principle, of love to God and love to man; which makes its followers do unto others as they themselves would be done by. If you demand liberty to yourself, it says, grant it to your neighbors.
>
> — DOUGLASS (1855, 415-16)

While the positive case for anti-slavery is that no one would choose slavery for themselves, and therefore it was wrong, Douglass also argued that slavery was wrong for other reasons:

I have shown that slavery is wicked—wicked, in that it violates the great law of liberty, written on every human heart —wicked, in that it violates the first command of the decalogue—wicked, in that it fosters the most disgusting licentiousness—wicked, in that it mars and defaces the image of God by cruel and barbarous inflictions—wicked, in that it contravenes the laws of eternal justice, and tramples in the dust all the humane and heavenly precepts of the New Testament.

— DOUGLASS (1855, 437)

How did the debate end? After the Emancipation Proclamation of 1863, and subsequent victory for the abolitionists, the debate seems to have faded away. Slavery was no longer an urgent issue to pursue by either side. The problems with just using a 'plain-sense' approach to scripture, without considering the trajectory or spirit of scripture, were forgotten.

How is that relevant to current debates over sexuality and gender? I think there are a few lessons we need to keep in mind. Before I outline these, some of you will be saying, 'but the issues are different'. And you would be right.

We cannot do a direct, one-for-one comparison between slavery and issues around sexuality and gender. But there are some points of overlap, and we can learn from these as we approach our current debate.

First, relying on just a 'plain-sense' approach to some specific verses is not how we should interpret the Bible. Adherence to this approach led many biblical scholars astray in the nineteenth century, leading to their failure to condemn slavery. The issues of slavery and sexuality and gender challenge how we should read and interpret scripture.

Secondly, our experiences have a part to play, and can give us insight into scripture. It was their personal experience of enslavement that led both Equiano and Douglass to read the Bible as being on the side of the enslaved; to realise and affirm the importance of liberty and equality. Experience can enable us to detect or appreciate parts of the Bible that others have missed or underplayed.

Third, and as a corrective to 'plain-sense', it is vital that we try to appreciate and understand the culture in which a Biblical text arose. What was the particular problem or issue that it was addressing? Some parts of the Bible are addressing specific, temporary issues, and to take them as timeless truths is to do a disservice to the Bible.

Appreciating that Biblical texts need to be understood within their historical contexts has always been a part of the evangelical tradition. However, it got lost during the debates over slavery. The principle applied was that if slavery was allowed or sanctioned at one point in history then it should always be accepted, in other words, as a timeless truth. Abolitionists, in contrast, saw the New Testament approach as containing the seeds leading to abolition, with room for owners as a temporary, time and culture-bound allowance.

This leads to the fourth point, which is that we must take not only specific verses seriously, but also the trajectory, or spirit ,of scripture. Failure to consider this aspect seriously enough is what led to a legalistic approach that allowed slavery.

What does it look like to try and apply these lessons to the current debates? Here is a brief, but not comprehensive, response.

First, the existence of a handful of verses that seem to prohibit homosexuality directly is not enough to decide the debate. White evangelicals also pointed to specific verses to prop up slavery as an institution.

Secondly, people who are LGBTQI+ need to be part of the discussion, and listened to carefully. It was those most directly affected by mis-readings in the slavery debate who provided different interpretations of scripture, which showed it could not be considered to be in favour of slavery. Similarly, in the current debates, the actual experience and reading of the Bible by people directly affected is essential. There is a famous slogan (with its roots in democratic reforms): *nothing about us without us.*

I am guilty here myself. This is a book written by a straight, cis-gendered white male, with multiple layers of structural advantage. However, I have consulted with people who are LGBTQI+, and tried to ensure that I am representing arguments that they too wish to make.

But too often, decisions are made in church meetings or synods by people without any experience, and without any challenge to one particular interpretation of the Bible. The slavery debates show the dangers inherent in that approach. Any discussions or debates about how to interpret the Bible on these issues must include those who are LGBTQI+.

Thirdly, we need to consider seriously the context of the verses that are often brought up. I hope that this book will help with this in a small way by bringing some of the scholarship to a wider audience. We are treading on treacherous ground if we simply assume that any and all statements in the Bible are timeless truths, rather than God at work in a particular time and place. Again, I do not want to be misunderstood. I do believe there are some timeless truths (for example: God is love; love your neighbour). But too often the cultural background of a verse is ignored and the reason for its place in the Bible dismissed. We do no favours to the Bible or ourselves when we treat it this way.

The fourth and final point is around the trajectory and spirit of scripture. Those who are non-affirming may also claim that they take this seriously. They present a narrative of a God who made male and female in creation, then uses a marriage metaphor for the relationship between Christ and the church. It is a serious response.

However, you can also see an affirming trajectory in scripture. God creates a world with amazing diversity, and proclaims it good. God creates a companion for the first human, because it is not good for humans to be alone. And our understanding of the scope of God's grace widens through Christ to include people who are considered unclean, and who do unclean acts and eat unclean foods. All of the amazing diversity of both humankind and creation is brought together in Christ, in whom there is no male and female.

Once you are aware of the trajectory, you start noticing it in scripture beyond the account in Acts 10–15 (another reason to include those with experience). For example, consider the account of the Syrophoenician woman (Mark 7:24–30). Jesus bluntly challenges this Gentile woman seeking help for her daughter, but her rejoinder shows why Jesus aids her:

> Jesus said to her, "Let the children be fed first, for it is not fair to take the children's food and throw it to the dogs." But she answered him, "Sir, even the dogs under the table eat the children's crumbs."
>
> — MARK 7:27–28

Cannot those who are LGBTQI+ eat the crumbs from under the table?

There are now two thousand years of Christian history. In that time, the Church has done much that is good, and some that is shameful. At various moments, Christians have been faced with choosing between an option seemingly prohibited by some scriptural verses, or considering the spirit of scripture and seeing God at work. On the issue of circumcision for Gentile males, an expansive reading of scripture won the day. On the issue of lending money at interest, an expansive reading of scripture won the day. On the issue of slavery, an expansive reading of scripture won the day.

This does not automatically mean that affirming the inclusion of people who are LGBTQI+ is right. But it should, at the very least ,make us humble and hesitant before declaring that it must be wrong. Consider whether, on the issue of affirmation, an expansive reading of scripture should win the day.

CHAPTER 14
CONCLUSION

IN THE BOOK of Judges 12:1–6, there is an account of a conflict between the Gileadites under Jephthah and the Ephraimites. The Gileadites defeat the Ephraimites, and the losing army scatters. The Gileadites control the escape back to Ephraim at the river Jordan. As people come to ford the river, the soldiers must identify any enemy fugitives. So, they ask them to say the word 'shibboleth' (which can mean a head of wheat, but can also mean stream).

How the people pronounce the word decides their fate. If they pronounce it 'sibboleth', it identifies them as the enemy, the Ephraimites, and they are killed by the soldiers. The word itself is not of particular importance, but as a mark of belonging, it identifies who is the enemy.

Sadly, in many ways the issues around sexuality and gender have become a shibboleth. Your views become a quick way of identifying to others whether or not you count as an evangelical, or even as a Christian. The issue is important mostly as an identity marker. The symbol, rather than the substance, is the focus.

We need to consider what makes someone an evangelical. We could do this in two ways. One would be to look sociologically. If we did this, we would consider evangelicals as a group. There may be group characteristics, such as what music is used in worship, how people pray, what conferences people go to, even what clothes people wear.

Groups guard boundaries: who is in, and who is not. And expressing an affirming position on sexuality or gender is in danger of marking you as not belonging—a modern day shibboleth.

But there is another way to consider what evangelical means. This is to focus on the substance of what and how evangelicals have worshipped and practised their faith. One approach to looking at evangelicalism is to focus on four areas:

- Conversion;
- The Bible;
- The cross;
- Being active in one's faith.

In the early days of the debates around gender and sexuality, some of those from the affirming position were not evangelicals. Therefore, they therefore tended to ignore the Bible. It is no surprise that some evangelicals found this lacking.

But that is not the case anymore. This book presents an affirming approach that takes the Bible seriously, based on the most relevant scholarship. Too many evangelicals never hear that you can both affirm scripture and also affirm the inclusion of people who are LGBTQI+. In this book, you have seen how the two do not need to contradict each other. You can maintain a high view of scripture and be affirming.

To return to those four marks, you can be affirming and still emphasise the importance of conversion, the inspiration of scripture, the centrality of the cross, and the calling to work out our faith in fear and trembling.

The main reason that many evangelicals believe that they

must remain non-affirming (beyond the power of it being a shibboleth) is because of a handful of verses in the Old and New Testament, which they have been taught apply in particular to people who are gay. .

This book has shown how a 'plain' reading of scripture in this area is dangerous. Our understanding of sexuality and gender is different from that of the cultures in which the Bible was written. It can lead us to misread and misinterpret that handful of verses.

In particular, sexuality in those cultures focused on dominance rather than on gender. The most common form of male same-sex intercourse involved abusing others, typically boys, who were usually enslaved, prostitutes or both. The other arenas for such intercourse, according to the rhetoric of the day, were the temples, where worship of fertility goddesses was said to include orgiastic rites.

Faithful, committed, monogamous, equal relationships between two men or two women were not what people were discussing or considering within the cultures. This is not to say that such partnerships did not exist, but that they would have been rare and not part of mainstream thought or experience.

This is the background needed when we come to the Bible verses. It means that where they imply male-male intercourse, it makes sense to assume that it refers to the most common forms of such intercourse within that culture. This is confirmed by more explicit concerns in the early church with pederasty.

In simple terms, the Bible is not talking about what we are talking about. The Bible is talking about pederasty, rape and orgies; we are concerned with loving relationships.

We also need to be careful in how we read the Bible when we consider people who are transgender. The Bible does not address transitioning, despite some people's confident, but mistaken, assertions that it does. Even taken on their own terms, the arguments of those who are against transitioning are weak and contradictory.

While our questions around sexuality or gender may not be addressed in the Bible directly, that does not mean that anything goes, or that we can say nothing. Scripture gives us a clear framework for our ethical decisions: love. Do our decisions and actions build others up? Do we see good fruit coming from these actions? Do we see bad fruit from a denial of possibilities?

When we apply these broader biblical principles to our issues, I believe a clear answer emerges.

In short, I cannot see how it is loving to deny the possibility of lifelong, faithful relationships to people of the same gender, to proclaim homosexuality as inherently sinful, or to insist that people try to change their gender identity to fit their physical bodies. The fruit of such approaches are rotten; what results is human misery.

The harm is to those who identify as LGBTQI+, who are sometimes given the false choice of imposed celibacy, denying their own identity, or walking away from the church.

It is easy for the church not to see this harm, as it is often hidden. Those who leave never get to tell their stories. The church never hears of their anger, bitterness or grief. Those left behind remain unchallenged.

And those who stay, also often suffer harm. Perhaps they try to suppress their desires, or worse still, find themselves encouraged, or forced, to undergo 'conversion therapy', with the psychological scars it leaves behind.

Acceptance, they learn, is strictly conditional.

But the harm is also to the church. We are meant to be a light to society. Instead, we are considered ignorant and unjust. Talking about sexuality or gender becomes an embarrassment. People are astonished at our teaching. Some churches stop talking about sexuality, because they know people will find the church's position immoral. Websites are coy about the actual beliefs or practices of the church.

You may hear that the church is meant to be countercultural. It is, but not for its own sake. Sometimes, being different from society just means that we have got it wrong.

And that means that the harm is also to society at large, who will not listen to the good news of God's love from what they consider to be a prejudiced organisation.

It is time to change. It is time to include, to affirm, to push up our chairs and ensure that all can have a seat at the table, rather than scrabbling in the dust for crumbs.

It is time to say yes to scripture, and yes to those who are LGBTQI+.

It is time to be affirmative.

POSTSCRIPT

You have read the book. What comes next? Can I suggest you consider your own answers to two questions? The first is this.

Where do you now stand personally?

Of course, you may still not know where you stand. Many of us find these areas complex, with various factors to consider and weigh. That is fine. It is OK not to be sure. Our world currently pushes us quickly into 'us' and 'them', with conflict and binary opposites good for ratings, clicks and likes.

And that leads to the second question.

What different viewpoints on these subjects can you accept as legitimate (even if you decide that they are, in your eyes, wrong)?

For the foreseeable future, I expect this area to remain one where there is disagreement. But I hope that we can live with Christians with whom we disagree.

APPENDIX

IF YOU WANT to study this issue further, I have included some pointers to relevant research or resources for some of the chapters in the book. I have kept it to a handful of the most important articles or books covering each topic. A fuller bibliography can be found at the website I maintain:

www.bibleandhomosexuality.org/bibliography/

Chapter 2: What does the Bible say about homosexuality?

The standard book on homosexuality and the Roman empire is by Williams. The first chapter in particular outlines the vastly different ways from today in which sexuality was understood and expressed. Ruden is also good on the horrific sexual culture of ancient Rome.

Ruden, Sarah. *Paul among the People: The Apostle Reinterpreted and Reimagined in His Own Time*. New York: Image Books, 2010.

Williams, Craig. *Roman Homosexuality*. 2nd ed. Oxford: Oxford University Press, 2010.

Chapter 3: How should we apply the Bible when our culture is different?

You can find Calvin's letter about moneylending to his friend Claude de Sachin at:

Calvin, John. *De Usuris*. Ioannis Calvini: Opera Quae Supersunt Omnia. Vol. 10. Edited by Guilielmus Baum, Eduardus Cunitz and Eduardus Reuss. Brunsvigae: C. A. Schwetschke, 1871.

Calvin's works are available through the University of Geneva.

You can find a summary of Calvin's approach, and its relevance to today, in an article by Andrew Goddard:

Goddard, Andrew. "Semper Reformanda in a Changing World: Calvin, Usury and Evangelical Moral Theology." In *Alister E McGrath and Evangelical Theology: A Dynamic Engagement*, edited by Sung Wook Chung, 235–63. Carlisle: Paternoster Press, 2003.

It is available on the Fulcrum website.

Others have also analysed Calvin's approach to money-lending—for example:

Wykes, Michael. "Devaluing the Scholastics: Calvin's Ethics of Usury." *Calvin Theological Journal* 38 (2003): 27–51.

Chapter 4: Adam and Steve (and Eve and Niamh)

In the chapter I refer to the Mishnah. This is a collection of oral laws that dates from around AD200, though it includes traditions far older. There are debates about how much these were observed by ordinary Jews, and also how far these applied in the time of Jesus and Paul (the Jewish rebellion of AD66 and the Roman reaction are significant in shaping Judaism).

I use the extracts from the Mishnah (m.Yevamot 6.6) to show how it is possible to take Genesis as prescriptive, and where the logic of that leads. The critical edition is:

Penka, Gabriele, *Die Mischna: textkritische Ausgabe mit deutscher Übersetzung und Kommentar*, Jevamot (Schwägerinnen), Jerusalem, 2009.

I also refer to Thomas Aquinas' argument that the command to be fruitful applied to the whole of humankind rather than every individual. The reference is:

Aquinas, *Summa Theologicae* 2.152.2.

Aquinas is part of a long Christian tradition that has never seen marriage and procreation as obligatory. It is a tradition that, of course, goes back to Paul and Christ.

Chapter 5: Leviticus, commandments and a new commandment

I give a broad overview within the chapter of how to approach Leviticus. Within each area, there is a whole realm of specialist literature. Particular understandings are sometimes contested.

For example, there is debate over whether Lev. 18:22 is primarily addressed to the 'active' partner (the one penetrating) or to the 'passive' partner (the one penetrated), and the reasons for the inclusion of the prohibitions in Leviticus. Olyan argues that the verses refer specifically to anal intercourse, not other types of male-male sexual activity, and that the verses originally addressed the penetrator.

Walsh disagrees, arguing that it is the penetrated who is addressed. Specifically, the law addresses free-born Israelite male citizens who take on voluntarily the role of the penetrated. He argues that this brings the law into closer conformity with expectations in ancient Rome and Greece, where it was also seen as shameful for a freeborn male to take on the role of the penetrated. See:

Olyan, Saul M. ""And with a Male You Shall Not Lie the Lying Down of a Woman": On the Meaning and Significance of Leviticus 18:22 and 20:13." *Journal of the History of Sexuality* 5, no. 2 (1994): 179–206.

Walsh, Jerome T. "Leviticus 18:22 and 20:13: Who Is Doing What to Whom?" *Journal of Biblical Literature* 120, no. 2 (2001): 201–09.

Between them, they lay out a range of possibilities for why the prohibitions existed. These include:

- association with temple prostitution;
- failure to act in conformity with the class 'male';
- impurity through mixing two bodily fluids (semen and excrement);
- failure to have intercourse in a way that is procreative;
- taking on a socially shameful role as the penetrated partner.

More recently, Töyräänvuori has questioned whether the verses refer to two males having intercourse together at all. She argues that the verses refer to the practice of two men having intercourse simultaneously with the same woman, and that the motive for the prohibition was to prevent children of uncertain parentage, who would therefore pollute the land. The argument is laid out in this article:

> Töyräänvuori, Joanna. "Homosexuality, the Holiness Code, and Ritual Pollution: A Case of Mistaken Identity." *Journal for the Study of the Old Testament* 45, no. 2 (2020): 236-67.

There is also much debate over whether male temple prostitutes, or indeed any temple prostitutes, ever existed in reality. For a forcefully argued thesis that sacred prostitution never existed, see in particular:

> Budin, Stephanie Lynn. *The Myth of Sacred Prostitution in Antiquity*. Cambridge: Cambridge University Press, 2008.

Whether or not they existed in reality, it remains the case that they existed in rhetoric—that is to say, that accusations of sacred prostitution were made in antiquity. To this extent, whether or not nations surrounding Israel did or did not practise sacred prostitution is less important for understanding Leviticus than whether Leviticus, and its audience, assumed or asserted that they did.

The conservative commentator Robert Gagnon assumes in his treatment that sacred prostitution did exist. He also assumes that this is at least part of the background to Lev. 18:22 and 20:13:

> I do not doubt that the circles out of which Lev 18:22 was produced had in view homosexual cult prostitution, at least

partly. Homosexual cult prostitution appears to have been the primary form in which homosexual intercourse was practiced [*sic*] in Israel.

— GAGNON (2001, 130)

However, he argues that as this would be the most acceptable context for male-male intercourse, banning cultic prostitution would be to ban all homosexual practice. I find his logic odd here. Cultic practices might have been the highest form for surrounding nations, but for Israel, and in particular the Holiness code in Leviticus, anything associated with idolatry is utterly unacceptable, which is what we would expect. His argument just does not work.

To demonstrate this, let us consider another practice prohibited by Leviticus and within the Holiness code—tattoos. Lev. 19:28 reads:

You shall not make any gashes in your flesh for the dead or tattoo any marks upon you: I am the LORD.

— LEV. 19:28

The prohibition on tattoos is universal. Why might it exist? Four main reasons have been given:

- that it is associated with pagan practices of mourning for the dead (as making gashes in the flesh in the first part of the verse);
- that it is associated with idolatry (tattoos proclaiming gods or goddesses or associated with religious practices);
- that it was associated with slavery (some enslaved people were tattooed); or

- that it defiled the body given in creation by God.

If it is one of the first two contexts, as many commentators suggest, then tattooing for religious reason would be the most acceptable context, which parallel Gagnon's argument. This would lead us to understand, using Gagnon's logic, that tattoos must be particularly awful in their own right if even religious use was prohibited. But the logic is the reverse—tattoos are prohibited precisely because of, and not despite, their links with paganism or with slavery. Gagnon's argument fails.

For more on tattoos and Leviticus, see:

Huehnergard, John, and Harold Liebowitz. "The Biblical Prohibition against Tattooing." *Vetus Testamentum* 63, no. 1 (2013): 59–77.

Gagnon primarily argues that the commands are there to prevent violation of gender complementarity; a distortion of gender. The lack of reference to females is problematic for this interpretation, and it remains speculative at best, despite how strongly he words his conclusions.

Gagnon, Robert A. J. *The Bible and Homosexual Practice: Texts and Hermeneutics.* Nashville: Abingdon Press, 2001.

Whilst all of these issues need addressing, the fundamental point remains that Christians do not look to Leviticus to order their lives.

At this point, some may argue that I am simply ignoring Leviticus entirely. Isn't it scripture? The argument, laid out more precisely by Tobias Haller, is this:

So the argument is not, "Since we have tossed out one biblical law we can toss out any law," but rather, "Since we have discerned that we are no longer bound by a law clearly labeled as belonging to a particular category of offense by Scripture itself, can we consider if we are also able to feel ourselves no longer to be bound by another commandment with exactly the same label."

— HALLER (2009, 90-91)

Haller, Tobias Stanislaus. *Reasonable and Holy: Engaging Same-Sexuality*. New York: Seabury Books, 2009.

The important command in Leviticus is the one Jesus and Paul refer to:

You shall love your neighbour as yourself.

— LEV. 19:18

Chapter 6: The sin of Sodom

Here is a list of occurrences of Sodom in the Bible, including deuterocanonical books, after its destruction in Genesis 19:

- Deuteronomy 29:23; 32:32
- Isaiah 1:9; 1:10; 3:9; 13:19
- Jeremiah 23:14; 49:18; 50:40
- Lamentations 4:6
- Ezekiel 16:46; 16:48; 16:49; 16:53; 16:55; 16:56
- Amos 4:11
- Zephaniah 2:9
- 3 Maccabees 2:5
- 2 Esdras 2:8; 7:106

- Matthew 10:15; 11:23; 11:24
- Luke 10:12; 17:29
- Romans 9:29
- 2 Peter 2:6
- Jude 7
- Revelation 11:8

One dimension I did not raise in the chapter is that Sodom's sin is a violation of hospitality. Hospitality was a key virtue in the Ancient Near East culture to an extent often unrecognised in the West.

Sodom should have welcomed Lot, and in turn welcomed his visitors. Instead, they tried to gang-rape both the visitors and Lot (note in particular Gen. 19:9 where Lot is singled out as an alien).

This failure of hospitality may lie behind passages such as Luke 10:12. It is in the context of a town's inhospitality to the seventy disciples sent out by Jesus that a comparison with Sodom is made.

Other interpretations of Genesis 19 are also possible. Meg Warner has pointed out that the account can be read as a misunderstanding between Lot and the men of the town. The citizens are angry at Lot for inviting strangers to stay overnight within the city, and want to 'know' who these strangers are. Lot understands them to want to know sexually, and so offers his daughters as he will not violate the hospitality he has offered to the angels. Morschauser makes a similar argument, but also suggests that Lot was not offering his daughters sexually, but as hostages overnight as a pledge of his own guarantee of the visitors. You can follow their readings in more detail here:

Morschauser, Scott. "'Hospitality', Hostiles and
   Hostages: On the Legal Background to Genesis 19.1–

9." *Journal for the Study of the Old Testament* 27 (2003): 461–85.

Warner, Meg. "Were the Sodomites Really Sodomites? Homosexuality in Genesis 19." In *Five Uneasy Pieces: Essays on Scripture and Sexuality*, edited by Nigel Wright. Adelaide: ATF Theology, 2011.

Chapter 7: The silence of the gospels

The root of the argument that *porneiai* in Mark 7:21–23 refers to Levitical offences appears to come from Gagnon, 191–93. For a relatively full response, see Haller, 125–134. A fairly comprehensive account of the development of the term *porneia* was provided by Harper. However, note that Glancy has argued that intercourse with one's own enslaved people would not necessarily have been seen by Jewish males as *porneia*.

Gagnon, Robert A. J. *The Bible and Homosexual Practice: Texts and Hermeneutics*. Nashville: Abingdon Press, 2001.

Glancy, Jennifer A. "The Sexual Use of Slaves: A Response to Kyle Harper on Jewish and Christian Porneia." *Journal of Biblical Literature* 134, no. 1 (2015): 215–29.

Haller, Tobias Stanislaus. *Reasonable and Holy: Engaging Same-Sexuality*. New York: Seabury Books, 2009.

Harper, Kyle. "Porneia: The Making of a Christian Sexual Norm." *Journal of Biblical Literature* 131, no. 2 (2012): 363–83.

For a similar perspective to mine on the nature of the relationship between the centurion and his slave, see the post 'A Centurion and his "Lover": a Text of Queer Terror' by Christopher Zeichmann. He has also addressed other aspects of this pericope in:

Zeichmann, Christopher B. "Rethinking the Gay Centurion: Sexual Exceptionalism, National Exceptionalism in Readings of Matt. 8:5–13//Luke 7:1–10." *The Bible and Critical Theory* 11 (2015): 35–54.

Chapter 8: Reading Romans the right way

The best general background to the world of Roman sexuality, especially in relation to homosexuality, is provided by Craig Williams, which highlights some of the differences from Ancient Greece covered in Dover's ground-breaking work. Karras also provides a helpful review of the evidence. Were there any homosexual partnerships in the modern sense that show any traces in the sources? Not many at all, but for potentially gay relationships, see Hubbard's review of peer homosexuality. For female partnerships, see Brooten (though I disagree with her interpretation of Romans 1).

Brooten, Bernadette J. Love between Women: Early Christian Responses to Female Homoeroticism. Chicago: University of Chicago Press, 1996.

Hubbard, Thomas K. "Peer Homosexuality." In *A Companion to Greek and Roman Sexualities*, edited by Thomas K. Hubbard, 128–49. Oxford: Wiley-Blackwell, 2013.

Karras, Ruth Mazo. "Active/Passive, Acts/Passions: Greek and Roman Sexualities." *The American Historical Review* 105, no. 4 (2000): 1250–65.

Williams, Craig. *Roman Homosexuality*. 2nd ed. Oxford: Oxford University Press, 2010.

Resources on 'against nature' and 'females'

More scholars are now questioning strongly whether or not Romans 1:26 refers to unnatural acts with other females or with males. Some of the key work here was done by Miller, both in his 1995 article and his 1997 rebuttal of Smith (1996). See also Swancutt, Banister and Lamas Jr. Looking at interpretations of Romans, de Bruyn notes that the fourth century Ambrosiaster initially interprets Romans 1:26 as involving women having unnatural relations with men.

The meaning of 'against nature' as being excessive desire is forcefully argued by Dale Martin, who also critiques many traditional interpretations of Romans. Swancutt also follows this line in her interpretation.

Banister, Jamie A. "Ὁμοίως and the Use of Parallelism in Romans 1:26–27." *Journal of Biblical Literature* 128, no. 3 (2009): 569–90.

de Bruyn, Theodore. "Ambrosiaster's Interpretations of Romans 1:26–27." *Vigiliae Christianae* 65, no. 5 (2011): 463–83.

Lamas Jr, Mark. "The Sin of Cunnilingus." In *Centre for the Study of Christian Origins*, edited by Helen Bond, Paul Foster, Larry Hurtado, Timothy Lim, Matthew Novenson, Sara Parvis, Philippa Townsend and Margaret Williams. Edinburgh: New College, University of Edinburgh, 2017.

Martin, Dale B. "Heterosexism and the Interpretation of Romans 1:18–32." *Biblical Interpretation* 3, no. 3 (1995): 332–55.

Martin, Dale B. *Sex and the Single Savior: Gender and Sexuality in Biblical Interpretation.* Louisville: Westminster John Knox, 2006.

Miller, James E. "The Practices of Romans 1:26: Homo-

sexual or Heterosexual." *Novum Testamentum* 37, no.
1 (1995): 1–11.

Miller, James E. "Response: Pederasty and Romans 1:27:
A Response to Mark Smith." *American Academy of
Religion* 65, no. 4 (1997): 861–66.

Smith, Mark D. "Ancient Bisexuality and the Interpretation of Romans 1:26–27." Journal of the American
Academy of Religion 64, no. 2 (1996): 223–56.

Swancutt, Diana M. ""The Disease of Effemination":
The Charge of Effeminacy and the Verdict of God
(Romans 1:18–2:16)." In *New Testament Masculinities*,
edited by Stephen D. Moore and Janice Capel
Anderson. Atlanta: Society of Biblical Literature,
2003.

Resources on pagan temple worship

The most comprehensive account is given in two articles by
Jeramy Townsley, which cover the rhetoric around pagan
temple worship as a background to Romans 1:26–27, and then
also the early Christian interpretations of the passage, which
refer to pagan worship. Budin provides an argument that sacred
temple prostitution only ever existed in rhetoric and not reality.
See also the blogpost by Helen King on the mundane reality of
Roman worship.

Budin, Stephanie Lynn. *The Myth of Sacred Prostitution in
Antiquity*. Cambridge: Cambridge University Press,
2008.

King, Helen. "Temple Prostitution for Christians."
In *Shared Conversations*. https://sharedconversations.
wordpress.com/2016/08/14/temple-prostitution-for-
christians/, 2016.

Townsley, Jeramy. "Paul, the Goddess Religions, and

Queer Sects: Romans 1:23–28." *Journal of Biblical Literature* 130, no. 4 (2011): 707–28.

Townsley, Jeramy. "Queer Sects in Patristic Commentaries on Romans 1:26–27: Goddess Cults, Free Will, and "Sex Contrary to Nature"?" *Journal of the American Academy of Religion* (2012).

Other interpretations

There are other interpretations of Romans 1. Overlapping with what is covered in the chapter, Diana Swancutt argues that Paul is condemning active, 'masculine' women and passive, 'feminine' men. In a completely different take, Elliott argues that Paul is actually targeting the scandalous behaviour of Roman emperors. I am not entirely convinced, but was surprised by how persuasive I found his argument when I delved deeper.

Elliott, Neil. *Liberating Paul: The Justice of God and the Politics of the Apostle*. Minneapolis: Fortress Press, 2006.

Swancutt, Diana M. ""The Disease of Effemination": The Charge of Effeminacy and the Verdict of God (Romans 1:18–2:16)." In *New Testament Masculinities*, edited by Stephen D. Moore and Janice Capel Anderson. Atlanta: Society of Biblical Literature, 2003.

Excerpt from Wisdom of Solomon as an attack on pagan idolatry

This passage shows some parallels with Paul's attack on pagan idolatry in Romans 1. Note the reference to 'frenzied revels', and how this is part of the worship of idols, which then leads to a long list of other sins.

And this became a hidden trap for humankind, because
people, in bondage to misfortune or to royal authority, bestowed on objects of stone or wood the name
that ought not to be shared.

Then it was not enough for them to err about the
knowledge of God, but though living in great strife
due to ignorance, they call such great evils peace.

For whether they kill children in their initiations, or
celebrate secret mysteries, or hold frenzied revels
with strange customs, they no longer keep either
their lives or their marriages pure, but they either
treacherously kill one another, or grieve one another
by adultery,

and all is a raging riot of blood and murder, theft and
deceit, corruption, faithlessness, tumult, perjury,
confusion over what is good, forgetfulness of
favours, defiling of souls, sexual perversion, disorder
in marriages, adultery, and debauchery.

For the worship of idols not to be named is the beginning and cause and end of every evil.

For their worshipers either rave in exultation, or
prophesy lies, or live unrighteously, or readily
commit perjury;

for because they trust in lifeless idols they swear wicked
oaths and expect to suffer no harm.

— WISDOM 14:21–29 (NRSV)

Chapter 9: The context of Corinth

The articles that are most relevant to this topic are those by
Wright, Martin and Elliott. Wright gave strong arguments
that *arsenokoitēs* derived from Leviticus, referred generally to all
male-male intercourse, and proceeded to argue that it applied

to all male-male intercourse, which included but went beyond pederasty. However, the thought that it was a general term including pederasty rather than a synonym for pederasty seemed to be assumed rather than proved by Wright.

Martin's rejoinder also covers *malakos*, where he produces a strong argument that it is dangerous to go beyond a general 'effeminate'. Martin notes how *arsenokoitēs* is linked with economic vices (not picked up by Wright), and emphasises the danger in trying to determine the meaning of a word when we have flimsy evidence. Some readers may find Martin's conclusions uncomfortable, but his analysis seems sound.

Elliott provides a comprehensive overview of a range of factors and critiques a wide range of translations in different Bibles. Elliott also concludes that there is a lack of clarity about what Paul meant, but argues that, for *arsenokoitai,* Paul is more likely to have been attacking the prevalent abusive pederasty.

Malick argues (unconvincingly to me) that Paul was addressing all homosexual behaviour. Petersen was an early critic of translations using 'homosexual', and Scroggs was one of the first to articulate powerfully the argument that pederasty was meant.

Elliott, John H. "No Kingdom of God for Softies? Or, What Was Paul Really Saying? 1 Corinthians 6:9–10 in Context." *Biblical Theology Bulletin* 34 (2004): 17–40.

Malick, David E. "The Condemnation of Homosexuality in 1 Corinthians 6:9." *Bibliotheca Sacra* 150 (1993): 479–92.

Martin, Dale B. "Arsenokoités and Malakos: Meanings and Consequences." In *Biblical Ethics & Homosexuality: Listening to Scripture*, edited by Robert L. Brawley. Louisville: Westminster John Knox Press, 1996.

Petersen, William L. "Can Ἀρσενοκοῖται Be Translated

by "Homosexuals"?" *Vigiliae Christianae* 40 (1986):
187–91.

Scroggs, Robin. *The New Testament and Homosexuality.*
Philadelphia: Fortress, 1983.

Wright, David F. "Homosexuals or Prostitutes? The
Meaning of Αρσενοκοιται (1 Cor. 6:9, 1 Tim.
1:10)." *Vigiliae Christianae* 38 (1984): 125–53.

Chapter 10: Jude the obscure

The reading that Jude 7 refers to intercourse between humans
and angels can be found in a range of commentators. Here are a
couple:

> As the angels fell because of their lust for women, so the
> Sodomites desired sexual relations with angels. *sarkos heteras,*
> "strange flesh", cannot... refer to homosexual practice... it
> must mean the flesh of angels.

— BAUCKHAM (1983, 54)

Bauckham, Richard J. *Jude, 2 Peter*, Word Biblical
Commentary vol. 50. Waco, Texas: Word, Incorpo-
rated, 1983.

The author's point here is not that the male inhabitants of
Sodom sought to have sex with male visitors, but that they
sought relations with angelic beings of an entirely different
order.

— KRAFTCHICK (2002, 39)

Kraftchick, Steven J. *Jude 2 Peter*, Abingdon New Testament Commentaries. Nashville: Abingdon Press, 2002.

The translation of 1 Enoch that I used can be found here:

Knibb, Michael A. *The Ethiopic Book of Enoch: A New Edition in the Light of the Aramaic Dead Sea Fragments.* Oxford: Oxford University Press, 1978.

Chapter 11: What does the Bible say about transgender people?

I refer to some scientific statistics in the chapter. Below are some of the papers on which they are based. I give approximate figures as different approaches give different ranges. For example, under some measures people who are intersex make up over 1% of the population. When using different criteria this figure drops dramatically.

Similarly, the figure for the proportion of the population which is transgender varies depending upon when and where the study was done. Additionally, we should expect higher figures as a society becomes more tolerant of transgender people.

The range of figures for prevalence are outlined in some general studies that also includes information on other aspects:

Keo-Meier, Colton, and Christine M. Labuski. "The Demographics of the Transgender Population." In *International Handbook on the Demography of Sexuality,* edited by Amanda K. Baumle, 289–327. New York: Springer, 2013.

Zucker, Kenneth J., Anne A. Lawrence, and Baudewijntje P. C. Kreukels. "Gender Dysphoria in Adults." *Annual Review of Clinical Psychology* 12 (2016): 217–47.

The evidence for a biological component to gender identity comes from twin studies. If the cause is part genetic, we might expect identical twins to be more alike than non-identical twins, who broadly share the same social environment.

That is exactly what a number of twin studies have found, showing that genetics has a part to play in gender identity. For example:

> Diamond, Milton. "Transsexuality among Twins: Identity Concordance, Transition, Rearing, and Orientation." *International Journal of Transgenderism* 14 (2013): 24–38.

When it comes to brain structure, a number of different approaches have been taken, some showing more of an effect than others. The approaches and results are summarised in this paper:

> Smith, Elke Stefanie, Jessica Junger, Birgit Derntl, and Ute Habel. "The Transsexual Brain—a Review of Findings on the Neural Basis of Transsexualism." *Neuroscience & Biobehavioral Reviews* 59 (2015): 251–66.

Bible and being transgender

In the chapter, I briefly consider Deuteronomy 22:5. This article deals with the issues more closely:

> Vedeler, Harold Torger. "Reconstructing Meaning in Deuteronomy 22:5: Gender, Society, and Transvestitism in Israel and the Ancient near East." *Journal of Biblical Literature* 127, no. 3 (2008): 459–76.

Some biblical resources are beginning to appear for those

who are transgender or are interested in this area. Here are some of them:

Hartke, Austen. *Transforming: The Bible and the Lives of Transgender Christians*. Louisville, Kentucky: Westminster John Knox Press, 2018.

Herzer, Linda Tatro. *The Bible and the Transgender Experience*. Cleveland, Ohio: Pilgrim Press, 2016.

Hornsby, Teresa A., and Deryn Guest. *Transgender, Intersex, and Biblical Interpretation*, Semeia Studies vol. 83. Atlanta: SBL Press, 2016.

Finally, not strictly about the Bible and the general phenomenon of people who are transgender, but the lived experience of a transgender Christian:

Mann, Rachel. *Dazzling Darkness: Gender, Sexuality, Illness and God*. Glasgow: Wild Goose Publications, 2012.

Gender variant

The chapter does not seek to address the issues around people who would describe themselves as gender-variant, or other designations. The aim was to show that, *on their own terms*, the arguments against being transgender are poor.

There is a separate argument about what is sometimes called 'gender confusion', and how people who are intersex, transgender or gender-variant undermine some of the assumptions that lie behind this phrase.

Chapter 12: An inclusive Bible

Most critical commentaries and some journal articles cover the differing interpretations of the Apostolic Decree from the council of Jerusalem in Acts 15.

One of the first to use the Acts analogy in relation to the affirmation of people who are LGBTQI+ was Siker. He argues for using the inclusion of Gentiles in Acts as an analogy for the inclusion of "'non-abstaining' homosexual Christians". He notes limitations of the analogy, including the difference between an orientation, and being a Gentile. However, Siker still considers the analogy helpful, particularly given his experience of Spirit-filled Christians who are gay.

In contrast, Goddard carefully considers but rejects the arguments for using the inclusion of the Gentiles as a paradigm for inclusion of people who are LGBTQI+. His objections to this are twofold. First, because Acts 15 is about accepting certain people, not certain actions. You may be able to tell whom God accepts, but not what actions to God are therefore acceptable. Secondly, he argues that the prohibition on *porneia* (sexual immorality) may have included homosexual conduct. He believes this problem is deepened if there is a link to Leviticus 17–18.

Witherington gives strong reasons for doubting that the Decree does refer to Leviticus 17–18, and argues instead that it should be seen as prohibiting practices associated with pagan worship.

Outside of mainstream approaches, Instone-Brewer argues that the prohibition on strangling may have referred to the practice of infanticide. Savelle interacts with Instone-Brewer, acknowledging some of the strengths of this argument, but then giving a full critique, which he argues makes it unlikely that Instone-Brewer is correct.

Perry has made a variety of contributions. In the first Perry

(2009) argues that the issue in Acts was the halakhic status of Gentiles. Should they be treated as proselytes, or as resident aliens? Either way, it is still under the Torah's description of Gentile salvation. Gentiles may then not need to follow all the law, depending on whether the scope of the law applies to them. The apostolic decree simply sets out the Torah's law for the non-Jew. However, there are two categories of non-Jew: the *ger toshav* (resident alien) and the *ben Noach* (a broader category, where the expectation was repudiation of idols and associated sins). Perry argues (following Bauckham) that Acts suggests resident aliens was the intended meaning. Perry then explores a variety of approaches that could be used when applying this as an analogy. He argues that the complexity of the analogy has not been fully explored.

In his next article, Perry (2010) outlines the history, from the 1970s up until 2010, of the use of the inclusion of the Gentiles as an analogy. He identifies five key issues. First, the council set certain requirements on the Gentiles. What would the equivalent requirements be on LGBTQI+ people? Would it be monogamy, or celibacy? Secondly, the Torah already distinguished between Jews and Gentiles. Are there non-universal moral precepts at work? Thirdly, what is the nature of the change in teaching? Is it that homosexuality used to be immoral, but now is not, or is it that it was always moral, but only now we realise this? Fourthly, how much would the inclusion of the Gentiles be anticipated? Would a welcome today be a continuation of that inclusion, or a new change? Fifthly, Cornelius is both a Gentile but also a 'god-fearer'. What, or who, are the correct analogues to Cornelius?

Perry then considers various presentations, including those by Siker, Seitz and Goddard. In particular, he considers Goddard's critique based on the prohibition of *porneia*. Perry notes that the link between the decree and Leviticus 17–18 is weaker than Goddard presents, but also in any case the reasoning is faulty. This is for two reasons: first, it would imply that Christians today should only eat kosher meat; avoiding, for example, blood. And secondly Goddard has moved from analogical argument to direct argument.

Olson argues that analogical use of the decree must supplement, not supplant, its plain meaning. Olson responds to Perry (2010), and also notes Goddard, Taylor, and others. In particular, Olson reacts to Perry's criticism of Goddard that he took the analogy too literally. Of note is that Olson maintains that the prohibition against eating blood should still be in force, introducing arguments about health and spiritual safety of one's neighbour. He does allow, though, that given textual variation, it would be enough to follow three of the decrees. By affirming the full apostolic decree today, Olson argues that it therefore prohibits same-sex relationships. Olson argues that allowing same-sex intercourse would displace the original meaning, because of the prohibition on immorality, and is therefore not applicable. Olson goes on to try to apply this pastorally to a range of situations.

Perry (2012) also responds to Goddard and Olson. First, Perry critiques Goddard for focusing on the actual prohibitions of the decree. The point of the analogy for 'revisionists' is that the ethical norms can change. Acts 15 gives one possible pattern how, including criteria and process. No-one is arguing that Acts 15 directly endorses homosexuality; rather, it shows that because church teaching changed in one way, it can change again.

Perry goes on to describe 'authoritative analogies' such as often used in medical ethics or law, for example, Deuteronomy 19:5. These differ from other comparisons without any authoritative backing. Olson might have argued (but did not) that special constraints or continuity in interpretation must apply to such analogies. However, Perry points out that the opponents of James were probably convinced that, at the council in Acts 15,

James was simply displacing the plain sense of Amos in his quotation of the prophet.

Perry also critiques Olson's argument that there is no change in teaching; that this was simply clarifying how non-Jews should be instructed and behave, and equivalent to a rabbinic ruling on Torah demands. The implication, for Olson, is that the Church should follow halakhic reasoning today. However, Perry notes that Jewish halakhic approaches vary: there are conservative and reformed approaches as well as Orthodox, which all differ in their approach to homosexuality. Perry, therefore, notes that the issue about what is development of tradition and what is corruption of tradition will remain.

Perry goes on to consider what it means for a group to be a minority rather than a majority, and whether there is a special vocation for those who are LGBTQI+.

Separately, Taylor also critiques Goddard, arguing that Goddard neither takes fully into account the interpretative leap taken in the Council by James and the other apostles, nor the way that (if the decrees do refer to Leviticus) the Church has since not observed the decrees equally.

See in particular:

Goddard, Andrew. *God, Gentiles and Gay Christians: Acts 15 and Change in the Church*, Grove Ethics Series vol. E121. Cambridge: Grove Books Ltd, 2001.

Instone-Brewer, David. "Infanticide and the Apostolic Decree of Acts 15." *Journal of the Evangelical Theological Society* 52, no. 2 (2009): 301–21.

Olson, Jon C. "The Jerusalem Decree, Paul, and the Gentile Analogy to Homosexual Persons." *Journal of Religious Ethics* 40 (2012): 321–47.

Perry, John. "Are Christians the "Aliens Who Live in Your Midst"? Torah and the Origins of Christian

Ethics in Acts 10—15." *Journal of the Society of Christian Ethics* 29, no. 2 (2009): 157–74.

Perry, John. "Gentiles and Homosexuals: A Brief History of an Analogy." *Journal of Religious Ethics* 38 (2010): 321–47.

Perry, John. "Vocation and Creation: Beyond the Gentile-Homosexual Analogy." *Journal of Religious Ethics* 40 (2012): 385–400.

Savelle, Charles H., Jr. "Infanticide in the Apostolic Decree of Acts 15 Revisited." *Journal of the Evangelical Theological Society* 62, no. 3 (2019): 533–42.

Siker, Jeffrey S. "How to Decide?: Homosexual Christians, the Bible, and Gentile Inclusion." *Theology Today* 51, no. 2 (1994): 219–34.

Taylor, Simon. "An Invitation to the Feast: A Positive Biblical Approach to Equal Marriage." *Modern Believing* 58, no. 1 (2017): 41–53.

Witherington III, Ben. *The Acts of the Apostles: A Socio-Rhetorical Commentary*. Grand Rapids, Michigan: William B. Eerdmans, 1998.

Chapter 13: Learning from history

I refer to a few works from the nineteenth century, which are listed here. For a good summary of the debates in America over slavery and the Bible, see the article by Harrill.

Douglass, Frederick. *My Bondage and My Freedom*. New York and Auburn: Miller, Orton and Mulligan, 1855.

Equiano, Olaudah. "A Letter for the Public Advertiser, 28th April 1788 to the Rev. Mr. Raymund Harris, Author of the Book, Called "Scripture Researches on the Licitness of the Slave Trade"." *The Public Advertiser*, 1788.

Harrill, J. Albert. "The Use of the New Testament in the American Slave Controversy: A Case History in the Hermeneutical Tension between Biblical Criticism and Christian Moral Debate." *Religion and American Culture: A Journal of Interpretation* 10, no. 2 (2000): 149–86.

Hodge, Charles. "Slavery. By William E. Channing." *The Princeton Review* 8, no. 2 (1836): 268–306.

Thornwell, James Henley. The Rights and Duties of Masters: A Sermon Preached at the Dedication of a Church Erected in Charleston, S. C., for the Benefit and Instruction of the Coloured Population. Charleston, S.C.: Press of Walker and James, 1850.

Support services

Some of the material in this book deals with subjects such as rape and sexual assault. Here is a short list of some UK based support services.

NHS Choices—Help after rape and sexual assault

http://www.nhs.uk/Livewell/Sexualhealth/Pages/Sexualassault.aspx

Rape Crisis

Helpline: 0808 802 9999 (12–2:30 and 7–9:30pm)

rapecrisis.org.uk

Sexual Abuse Referral Centres—Find a SARC

http://www.nhs.uk/Service-Search/Rape%20and%20sex
ual%20assault%20referral%20centres/
LocationSearch/364

SARCs are specialist medical and forensic services for anyone who has been raped or sexually assaulted. They aim to be a one-stop service, providing the following under one roof: medical care and forensic examination following assault/rape and, in some locations, sexual health services. Medical Services are free of charge and provided to women, men, young people and children.

A NOTE ON LANGUAGE

Words are important. How we communicate has the power to heal and to hurt; to build up and to belittle; to dignify and to destroy.

Within this book, my intention is to use language which is not off-putting, rude or offensive to others.

However, I may have, on occasion, failed in this endeavour. If there are particular examples, please first accept my apologies, and secondly, if you are able to let me know, then I will try to update the book more appropriately.

Language also evolves, changing from one generation to another. Perhaps you are reading this book some years after it was first written. Again, please forgive me if some of the language has become offensive within your time and context.

I have attempted to use current (British) usage when referring to people who are LGBTQI+, and the contents have been read through by others in an effort to ensure that I have used appropriate language. My thanks go to these readers; any remaining errors are mine.

One problem is how to refer to those on different sides of the debates over sexuality and gender within Christianity. There are no neutral terms. In choosing language for those opposed to same-sex marriage and transitioning, 'traditionalist' implies that the Church has always had a view on these controversies, whereas in reality it is only in the last few decades that the Church has begun to grapple with sexuality and gender identity. 'Conservative' is perhaps less loaded, but tends to bring with it implications around a range of theological issues where those who are 'conservative' on sexuality may differ (for example, the role of women in ministry).

Terms for those in favour of accepting LGBTQI+ people and same-sex marriage are equally problematic. 'Progressive' implies that those who object do so because they are against progress. 'Revisionist' implies that the Church already has a thought-through position on the issue. 'Inclusive' is popular, but raises issues beyond sexuality and gender, and is objected to by those who do not wish to be defined as 'non-inclusive'.

I have therefore settled on 'affirming' and 'non-affirming', with the understanding that this is in relation to the acceptance of people who are LGBTQI+, including same-sex marriage.

I faced particular issues over the language of slavery, which is in the process of evolving as I write. Just a couple of years ago, terms such as 'master' and 'slave' were the default in writing about slavery. However, in ensuring that the dignity of the person is not erased or forgotten, there is a move to replace these terms with 'enslaver' and 'enslaved person'. This movement has, I believe, come from America where the history of slavery continues to impact the world of today, though this is true in a different way in Britain.

I have tried to use 'enslaved person' and similar terms throughout this book. The exceptions I have made are in biblical quotations, and in writing about the centurion's slave, because this so closely links to the biblical text.

I have continued in a variety of places to use the term 'master' as a translation for the male head of the household in Roman times, the *dominus*. The *familia* in the Roman empire was the basic unit of society, and the *dominus* as *paterfamilias* exercised legal power over both his children and enslaved persons. 'Enslaver' would not capture the extent of his legal power, and so I have retained 'master' for this context. I am aware that this is problematic, potentially encoding and reinforcing systems of domination, and would welcome feedback on better alternatives.

ACKNOWLEDGMENTS

The genesis of this book came from presentations and workshops for Baptist ministers in training at Northern Baptist College. These students came from a wide variety of backgrounds and traditions. Not all of them agreed with my viewpoint, but all of them helped improve the clarity of the material and ensured that common questions were answered.

Material has also been used in teaching a variety of postgraduate modules on the Bible. Again, students from diverse backgrounds have engaged with, critiqued and wrestled with working with the Bible and sexuality and gender. Their contributions have also helped to make this a better book.

The material has also been road-tested on a variety of church groups and ministers' groups over the years. Their contribution has also been invaluable.

A constant source of support has been my wonderful colleagues, past and present, at Northern Baptist College and the Luther King Centre for Theology and Ministry (formerly known as Luther King House). This support has ranged from co-teaching in this area (first with Kathy White, and more recently with Meg Warner), to enabling sabbatical cover, to generally making my environment a great place to work. This support has come from both academic and non-academic staff, and is appreciated.

My friend Giles has been supportive throughout, and has contributed to sessions on sexuality with ministers in training.

My thanks to Nicole Leann, who provided copy editing and

checked for appropriate language. Her professionalism helped improve the book; remaining errors are my responsibility

My family have both supported and encouraged me, and also kept me grounded throughout.

To all these people, and others who do not quite fit into these categories but nonetheless helped, thank you. The fact that the book is not as good as it could be is down to me. The fact that it is a lot better than it could have been is thanks to you.

COPYRIGHT - SCRIPTURAL PASSAGES

Milton Keynes UK
Ingram Content Group UK Ltd.
UKHW041458041123
431960UK00004B/219